The Kirtland's Warbler

The Story of a Bird's Fight Against Extinction
and the People Who Saved It

William Rapai

THE UNIVERSITY OF MICHIGAN PRESS : *Ann Arbor*

Published in the United States of America by
The University of Michigan Press
Manufactured in the United States of America
⊗ Printed on acid-free paper

2015   2014   2013   2012   4   3   2   1

A CIP catalog record for this book is available from the British Library.

Library of Congress Cataloging-in-Publication Data

Rapai, William.
    The Kirtland's warbler : the story of a bird's fight against
extinction and the people who saved it / William Rapai.
       p. cm.
    Includes bibliographical references and index.
    ISBN 978-0-472-11803-8 (cloth : alk. paper) — ISBN 978-0-472-
02806-1 (e-book)
    1. Kirtland's warbler.   2. Rare birds.   I. Title.
QL696.P2438R37 2012
598.168—dc23   2011032761

Text design and composition by
Mary Hurthal Sexton
Set in Perpetua, designed by Eric Gill, and
released by Monotype in 1932

To my mother, the science teacher . . .
It's all your fault!

The first rule of intelligent tinkering is to save all the pieces.

—ALDO LEOPOLD

Contents

Acknowledgments

Even though this section is called "Acknowledgments," it really should be called "Thank-Yous." That's because merely acknowledging people isn't good enough.

The list of people to thank for their assistance in helping me write this book is too long for me to include every single person, but know that I appreciate your contribution, no matter how small.

I would be remiss, however, if I did not take time to issue some special thanks.

Thank you to Dave Dempsey for suggesting that I write this book; Julie Craves for helping me to focus the concept; Mitch Zuckoff and Suzanne Kreiter for their insights, advice, and excellent breakfasts and dinners; and Janet Hinshaw for allowing me to pillage the documents of the bird collection at the University of Michigan Museum of Zoology.

Thank you to the people who reviewed sections of the book: Paul Aird, Anthony Allegrina, Larry Baker, Carol Bocetti, Elaine Carlson, Richard Carpenter, Julie Craves, Emily Everett, Dave Ewert, Greg Huntington, Phil Huber, Lisa Olsen, Ray Perez, Mike Petrucha, Barry Puckett, Sarah Rockwell, Richard Thompson Jr., Jerry Weinrich, and Joe Wunderle.

Thank you to my camping buddies, Tony, Barry, Dave, and Larry, for putting up with my need to roll out of bed before sunrise to get to an interview or some obscure intersection for the annual Kirtland's warbler census.

A special thank-you goes out to Maggie and Julia for their support over the past three years. Their excitement about their dad's project sustained me and kept me going when I wanted to throw the laptop against the wall.

Finally, I need to extend the biggest thank-you to the Lovely Joann for helping me to refocus when I strayed from the task, for giving me the proper word when I drew a blank, and for providing me with the strength and encouragement to complete this project. Joann, everything good in this book is because of you.

Introduction

The ornithologist Charles Pease had no idea what kind of bird he had just shot in northeastern Ohio on May 13, 1851, but he knew what to do with it: give it to his father-in-law, Dr. Jared Kirtland.

Kirtland was, by all accounts, an extraordinary man. As a child in Connecticut, he didn't show much interest in the games of his fellow schoolchildren. Instead, under the guidance of his grandfather, Dr. Jared Potter, Kirtland studied the Linnaean system of biology and learned how to observe and identify plants and animals and how to accurately record his observations and sightings.

After becoming one of the first students at Yale University's new medical school and graduating when he was only twenty-one, Kirtland went on to a long career as a practicing physician, a horticulturist, and, after moving to the Cleveland area, a cofounder of Case Western Reserve University's medical school and member of the Ohio legislature. He was also a collector of bird skins and an accomplished zoologist, authoring the first complete survey of the animals of Ohio.

But for all his knowledge, Kirtland could not identify this bird. He and Pease compared it to other species with which they were familiar. They quickly realized that even though this specimen bore a resemblance to magnolia and yellow-rumped warblers, it was too big and the field marks didn't match. This, they concluded, was something unique. But what was it?

As luck would have it, a few days later, Dr. Spencer F. Baird, a renowned bird biologist and assistant secretary of the Smithsonian

Institution, happened to be passing through Cleveland on his way back to Washington from a meeting in Cincinnati. Kirtland gave the skin of the unknown bird to Baird, who took it back to the museum.

The following year, Baird published an account of this new species in the *Annals of the Lyceum of Natural History of New York*. Running about a page and a half long, "Description of a New Species of Sylvicola," by S. F. Baird, featured a short description of the bird's overall appearance and dimensions and the lengths of the bill, hind toe, and second through sixth primary flight feathers.[1] Baird's account closes, "This species, which was shot near Cleveland, Ohio, by Mr. Charles Pease, May 13, 1851, is appropriately dedicated to Dr. Jared P. Kirtland, of Cleveland, a gentleman to whom, more than any one living, we are indebted for a knowledge of the Natural History of the Mississippi Valley."

Although Kirtland's name is now bound to this species forever, the bird might just as easily have been called Cabot's warbler—if only Dr. Samuel Cabot of Boston had realized what he had in his possession. While on a boat passing through the Bahamas in 1841, ten years before Pease aimed his shotgun at his specimen, Cabot shot a male Kirtland's warbler near Abaca Island. The story goes that Cabot became so engrossed by tropical birds he saw on the Yucatan Peninsula later on that same expedition that he forgot about the unidentified warbler, and the specimen languished in his collection for more than twenty years.

It seems odd that Cabot would let this specimen just sit in a drawer because as an ornithologist he was no slouch. On his trip to the Yucatan, he discovered the ocellated turkey (*Meleagris ocellala*) and thoroughly described several other bird species. Upon his death in 1885, he was lauded as a contemporary of John James Audubon and Thomas Nuttall, two giants who helped to revolutionize biological science through their studies of the plants and animals of the North American frontier in the early nineteenth century.[2]

Baird, Cabot, and Kirtland discovered the Kirtland's warbler at the time of an amazing expansion of human knowledge about the natural sciences. The Lewis and Clark expedition had been completed forty-five years earlier, and other explorers were scouring the American West to fill in the gaps. John James Audubon had published his *Birds of America* twenty years earlier, but the European public clamored for more information and illustrations of the exotic species of the New World. Charles Darwin was preparing his breakthrough book, *On the Origin of Species*. Great Britain's Charles Lyell's theories of uniformitarianism were becoming the basis of modern geology. Scientific societies and governments in England and France sent expeditions to survey the farthest reaches of the earth to bring plant and animal specimens back to museums in London and Paris.

In North America, the National Museum of Natural History in Washington, DC, the Academy of Natural Science in Philadelphia, and the New York Academy of Sciences were eagerly competing with each other to document the zoology of North America and create the best collections of plants and animals in the country. Museums at Harvard University and the University of Michigan were also making important contributions and building impressive collections. Any new species was greeted with great excitement, and those that were rare—like the Kirtland's warbler—were even more highly prized. Based on the number of specimens taken in the Bahamas in the late nineteenth and early twentieth centuries, it had become clear that this is where the warbler spent its winters. But where did the bird go each summer to nest and raise its young?

In the fifty years after Baird named the species, only a handful of Kirtland's warblers would be sighted or collected on the North American continent. Many of those would come from the Mississippi Valley region of Missouri, Illinois, and Minnesota. Those sightings led the ornithologist Frank Chapman to speculate in writing in October 1898 that the Kirtland's warbler's migratory route took the bird across the southern United States from the Bahamas to the Mississippi Valley and then north.[3] Furthermore, since one specimen was found dead after it had run into a lighthouse in the middle of Lake Huron on May 21, 1851, Chapman was certain that the bird was "doubtless en route to a more northern breeding ground in the Hudson Bay region."[4]

It's perhaps ironic then that the obscurity of the Kirtland's warbler (with some help from Chapman's errant speculation) may have helped save it.

No one in Chapman's day knew how many individual Kirtland's warblers existed, but ornithologists, collectors, and museum curators all knew they wanted a skin or an egg—or several—for their collections. Science, well into the twentieth century, was conducted at the end of a shotgun; if a species was going to go extinct, museums and collectors were going to do whatever they could to get a skin, even if it meant shooting the last bird. Certainly, hunting by professional collectors helped push the ivory-billed woodpecker over the edge and contributed to the decline of the piping plover.[5] In the case of the Kirtland's warbler, however, they couldn't collect what they couldn't find.

Luckily, that ethic has changed in the past hundred years. Over the past half century, at a time when the warbler teetered on the edge of extinction, hundreds of researchers, government biologists, and amateur ornithologists have worked feverishly to unlock the secrets of the Kirtland's warbler on its northern Michigan nesting grounds. Instead of hastening the bird toward extinction as would have been done by a previous generation, they have brought the species back. Researchers have discovered that the Kirtland's warbler is a discriminating creature and found innovative ways to meet its needs. From a total population estimated at four hundred birds in 1987, the Kirtland's warbler population had grown to more than thirty-five hundred by 2010. And with the Kirtland's warbler expanding its nesting range into Michigan's Upper Peninsula, Wisconsin, and Ontario, the population is poised to grow further. It now appears likely that the Kirtland's warbler will be removed from the federal Endangered Species List. And with the support of researchers, educators, private citizens, professional fundraisers, and government officials from the United States, Canada, and the Bahamas, the future of the Kirtland's warbler seems secure. No one, of course, is certain, because the Kirtland's warbler's story is one of boom and bust and just plain luck. Population swings have taken the bird close to extinction at least twice in the past fifty years. The first time it was pushed to the brink by nature, and humans unintentionally brought it back. The second time it was pushed to near extinction by humans, and an act of nature accidentally brought it back.

The truth is that the Kirtland's warbler is a "conservation reliant" species. It would not have survived to this point without human intervention in the form of intense habitat management and parasite control, and it will take that same intervention in order to ensure its future. It also took the cooperation of government agencies, businesses, and the people with whom the bird shares the northern woods. It took the insight of Norman Wood, the curator of birds at the University of Michigan Museum of Natural History, who traveled for three days from Ann Arbor by train, rowboat, and foot to discover the Kirtland's warbler's breeding ground along the Au Sable River. Josselyn Van Tyne, Harold Mayfield, and Lawrence Walkinshaw documented the bird's nesting habits and biology. Even Nathan Leopold, a brilliant young man who helped commit one of the most notorious murders of the twentieth century, made a significant contribution to the knowledge base by recording the warbler's activities at its nest and being among the first to note the threat posed by the brown-headed cowbird.

Later it was the work of a college professor who collected Kirtland's warbler droppings to be later analyzed to learn that the bird eats aphids and spittlebugs, among other things, and a private citizen who led a quixotic attempt to get the Michigan Legislature to name the Kirtland's warbler the state bird. Today it's a volunteer who keeps migration records, helps count the birds in an annual census, and leads field trips during an annual festival. It's a now retired research biologist who has kept tabs on the Kirtland's warbler population every year since 1973. It's the children in Michigan and the Bahamas who participate in an annual contest to get their drawings on a calendar. It's the government employees who act as ambassadors for the bird, building bridges with the suspicious and educating the interested.

Why do so many people find this bird a source of fascination? Why do so many care so much about it? It's not like the Kirtland's warbler is cuddly like a panda or cute like a baby seal. It doesn't provide an opportunity for cross-species kinship like a dog or demonstrate a capacity to learn amusing tricks like a captive orca. The Kirtland's warbler, however, is not without charisma. The male is a handsome bird, with a lemon-yellow breast, a blue-gray back, and an arc of white above and below his eyes. On a warm spring morning, he'll sit atop a pin oak branch and sing for hours. Nearly everyone who witnesses this display is charmed by the warmth of the warbler's song and the depth of his effort. Researchers who work with Kirtland's warblers on their nesting grounds talk openly of the admiration they have for the birds they have encountered. They tell amazing stories about how it seems that the warblers welcome humans into their world.

The real answer to the question of why so many people care is less aesthetic and more philosophical. The Kirtland's warbler is endangered because of human activity, and the bird's fans carry a sense of obligation to make things right. But many fans are also driven by a sense of pride. Until the warbler started nesting in Wisconsin in 2008, it was thought to be the only bird species that nested exclusively in Michigan.

To tell the story of the Kirtland's warbler is to tell a story of complex relationships between the bird and its environment, the bird and humans, and the bird and the state and federal governments' complex policies toward it. And just when it appears that the Kirtland's warbler has recovered for good and the boom and bust cycle is over, a policy change may send it into a downward spiral once again.

The Kirtland's warbler is often described as a "bird of fire" because of its preference for nesting in areas after a wildfire. But it just as easily could be called a bird of fire for the passion it ignites in the humans who have dedicated themselves to understanding and protecting the species. This book is the story of that unusual relationship.

PART ONE : *The Past*

ONE : The Jack-Pine Bird

For Alexander W. Blain Jr., the editor of the *Bulletin of the Michigan Ornithological Club,* the news from northern Michigan was a "Stop the presses!" moment.

Blain had already sent the June 1903 issue of the publication to the printers when he received word from Norman Wood, a taxidermist at the University of Michigan Museum of Natural History: the Kirtland's warbler was nesting in Michigan, and he had proof. The news was so big that Blain recalled the publication from the printer to append a two-paragraph note to the last page.

> Just after this issue had gone to press Mr. Wood returned home from his trip north in quest of the Kirtland's Warbler with very gratifying success, having obtained a fine series of skins, male, female, nestlings, full-fledged young, nest and eggs.
>
> Mr. Wood also obtained some two dozen photographs of the birds (in life) and their nests. The material of this trip prepared by Mr. Wood and illustrated by the photographs, will be given to our readers in the third issue. The editor also hopes to be able to give a colored plate of the egg. There shall also be articles on the rare and interesting bird by Chas. A. Adams, A.B. Covert and Earl H. Frothingham.[1]

Blain knew well that Wood's discovery was important. Fifty-two years had passed since Charles Pease shot his Kirtland's warbler near

Norman Wood, a taxidermist at the University of Michigan Museum of Natural History, discovered the nesting grounds of the Kirtland's warbler near northern Michigan's Au Sable River in 1903. Wood would later go on to become the curator of birds at the museum. He would tutor a brilliant young ornithologist, Nathan Leopold, who would also go on to study the warbler. (Courtesy of the Bentley Historical Library, University of Michigan.)

Cleveland, and the species was still an ornithological enigma. The question of where the Kirtland's warbler spent its winters had effectively been settled as collectors regularly took birds out of the Bahamas. But bigger, more important questions remained to be answered. What was the Kirtland's warbler's primary habitat? What was its migration route? And, most important, where did it nest?

Speculation in ornithological circles had become something of a parlor game. Some argued that the bird nested in northern Lower Michigan, Wisconsin, and Minnesota. Others argued for Michigan's Upper Peninsula. One ornithologist speculated that it was farther north still, in Canada near Hudson Bay, based on a single record of a Kirtland's warbler being killed when it ran into a lighthouse in Lake Huron.

In 1898, Frank Chapman, who is today considered the dean of American ornithologists, tried to bring what little was known about the Kirtland's warbler into perspective. In a brief article in the *Auk,* the prestigious journal of the American Ornithologists' Union (AOU), Chapman lamented that in the previous twenty years ornithologists had been able to discover the range of nearly every warbler species in North America. The lone exception, he wrote, was the Kirtland's warbler.[2]

Chapman laid out the few spring migration records from Missouri, Minnesota, Illinois, Indiana, Wisconsin, Michigan, Ontario, and Virginia and concluded, "These brief notes constitute our sole knowledge of the habits of this species, whose nest and eggs, owing to its rarity and the remoteness of its probable breeding range will doubtless remain long unknown."[3]

So, on June 29, 1903, with great anticipation, Wood boarded a train bound for Roscommon, Michigan, on the Toledo, Ann Arbor and Northern Railroad, knowing that he could be on the cusp of a breakthrough.

Wood went north in pursuit of the Kirtland's warbler after Earl Frothingham, a University of Michigan graduate student and museum employee, returned from a fishing trip in northeastern Michigan's Oscoda County with a gift: the corpse of an unknown species of bird. Frothingham reported seeing and hearing several of these unknown birds along the north side of the Au Sable River, and since he was unfamiliar with it he had his fishing companion shoot one for the museum. Wood identified the skin as that of a male Kirtland's warbler and immediately went to museum curator Charles Adams, who, in Wood's words, "also saw the importance of the discovery, and the necessity of sending a man to the spot at once."[4]

By today's standards, Wood's account of his trip to find the nesting area of the Kirtland's warbler is comical. Articles for modern peer-reviewed journals are almost reptilian in their cold-blooded and emotionless pursuit of fact. Wood's article, on the other hand, is a scientific paper, yes, but it's also a quirky travelogue and an expression of joyous emotion. Wood's account, printed in the March 1904 issue of the *Bulletin,* describes his travels by train to Roscommon ("I arrived at this old lumber town at 4 A.M. June 30th, after a tedious night's travel, due to two changes of cars"), by boat ("This country is wild and very interesting, and the songs of many birds cheered me, as with note-book in hand I floated along"), and on foot, describing the wildlife and geographical features he saw along the way.

At sunrise on July 2, Wood struck out on foot to find the spot where Frothingham had found the Kirtland's warbler. After crossing the Au Sable River and climbing a steep slope that opened into a young jack pine forest, he wrote:

> [S]uddenly I heard a new song, loud, clear, joyous and full of sweet melody. This song may be described as follows: *weche chee-chee-chee-chee-r-r-r.* . . . I thought it a Kirtland, although I had never before heard its song. I heard this song repeatedly at intervals of about 30 seconds, and from different directions. . . . I repeatedly tried to go where he sang last, and finally saw him flit from a bush to a yellow oak scrub and light about three feet above the ground. As I watched him he sat quite erect, threw forward his head and the wonderful song rang out. This song was remarkable because of its volume and rich melody. I was sure this was the bird for which I was in search; but in order to make certain the identity I shot it.[5]

Wood spent the next five days searching the area for a nest without luck. On July 8, he was riding in a horse-drawn carriage when he saw a Kirtland's warbler fly to a dead tree on the side of the road.

> This bird had a worm in his mouth, so I concluded that his nest was near by, and that he would go to it with the worm. I went to the side of a large stub, and while I was watching, saw this male assume the erect singing position, throw forward his head and try to sing, still holding the worm in his mouth. . . . Again he sang and wagged his tail and then dove down, but this time two rods to the west of the tree. I started to go there, when just south of the tree I flushed the female from the ground and after a close look, saw the nest. It may be imagined with what delight I beheld the first nest of this rare bird ever seen, and with what eagerness I dropped to my knees beside it to make a closer examination of its contents. There

were two young birds, perhaps ten days old, and a perfect egg; this proved to be the only egg found.

Wood described the nest as built in a depression on the ground, partially covered with blueberry and sweet fern plants, underneath a five-foot-tall jack pine tree.

Wood took thorough field notes of the structure and composition of the nest, the surrounding vegetation, and the condition of the young birds. Wood continued his studies for the next few days, noting that the birds were not shy around humans and that one female had briefly landed on the shoe of one of his companions. He shot several more male specimens and found at least one other nest, which he also studied closely. On July 11, Wood dug up that nest and the surrounding vegetation to ship back to Ann Arbor for further study.

> After getting a photograph of the nest and its vicinity I shot the pair of birds and kept the young alive. We dug up the nest and started for [the home of a local resident where Wood was staying], arriving after dark. I kept the young alive, by feeding them houseflies, until the 13th. Then they died, and I made skins of them, preserving the bodies. I had hoped to rear these young, at least to keep them alive until I reached Ann Arbor. I evidently did not have the variety of food required, although they ate from six to ten flies each at a time and then went to sleep very contentedly.

There was one other thing that Wood learned: even though the nesting location of the Kirtland's warbler had been unknown to science, the bird was very familiar to the people living in the area. They knew it simply as "the jack-pine bird."[6]

In his summary, Wood took a guess at estimating the size of the colony's population. "We may then estimate that the colony contained thirteen pairs of birds," he wrote, "with their increase, and assuming that each nest contained on an average four young, we have fifty-two young birds. Adding to this the number of the parents, twenty-six, gives an estimated total of seventy-eight (78) birds in the area described."

Wood's discovery was quickly acknowledged in the *Auk* by the American Ornithologists' Union.

The song and the habits of the birds as observed in their breeding haunts are minutely described, and descriptions and half-tone illustrations are given of the egg and nests, of the sites where the nests were found, and of the mounted group of these birds now in the Museum of the University of Michigan, prepared by Mr. Wood from the materials obtained on this expedition. Although preliminary notices of these discoveries have been published, this paper forms the most important contribution thus far made to the history of the species, which is at last removed from the small list of North American birds whose nests and eggs and breeding habits still remain unknown.[7]

The revelation also allowed ornithologists to open a new round of speculation about the Kirtland's warbler. The same issue of the *Bulletin* that featured Wood's account also included an article on the warbler's migration route written by Charles Adams, the curator of the University of Michigan Museum and Wood's boss. Adams argued that it was important to research and understand the species' migration route because it could reveal how the Kirtland's warbler had populated the Great Lakes region after the Wisconsin glacier receded. Adams speculated that the warbler had nested in the pines of the American Southeast while Michigan lay under tons of ice and that the migration route would have been a simple jump across the Gulf Stream from the Bahamas to the southeastern United States. But once the glacier receded and jack pines began to occupy the north, Adams argued, the warbler made its way northward by following its traditional migration route from the Bahamas to the southeastern United States and then to the Mississippi River via the southern pine barrens. Once the birds reached the Mississippi River, they turned north to reach the Ohio Valley about the first week in May and northern Ohio and southern Michigan in the second or third week of May. To reach the northern Michigan jack pines, Adams suggested that the bird would take the Mississippi to the Wabash River. It would then leave the river valley near Fort Wayne, Indiana, and travel over land to the Maumee River, which empties into Lake Erie at Toledo, Ohio. A Kirtland's warbler would then follow the shoreline of Lake Erie, the Detroit River, Lake St. Clair, and the St. Clair River to Lake Huron. Instead of crossing Saginaw Bay from Michigan's Thumb to Tawas Point, Adams speculated that the bird flew around the bay, following the shoreline.

Why this circuitous route? Adams cites the work of Frank Leverett, who had earlier documented ancient glacial lakes and drainage lines in the Mississippi River watershed that "form conspicuous features of the topography." If the Kirtland's warbler came north following the receding glaciers, Adams argued, it was only "natural that it would follow such highways . . ."[8]

It seemed reasonable that the Kirtland's warbler would follow the expanding territory of the pines as they followed the receding glacier. However Adams and Leverett were wrong. We now know that the pines didn't migrate up the Mississippi River watershed. The jack pine arrived in Michigan some 11,500 years ago, after it moved up the East Coast and then expanded west.[9] That expansion would make the jack pine's migration pattern much more consistent with the Kirtland's actual route to and from the Bahamas.

With so little known about the Kirtland's warbler in the early twentieth century, it's easy to see how Adams and Chapman could reach faulty conclusions about its migration route.

Wood's discovery of the Kirtland's warbler nesting grounds sent egg collectors, ornithologists, and museum workers into a frenzy; everyone wanted a skin or a nest or an egg. Wood used what few Kirtland's warbler skins he had as a bartering device, often garnering several bird skins for his museum in exchange for just one Kirtland's warbler. One of the first letters he sent was to Joseph Grinnell, the business manager of the *Condor,* a magazine of western ornithology based in Pasadena, California. In March 1904, Grinnell responded, "In reply to yours of Mar. 7th: I should be glad to get a first class pair of skins of Kirtland's warbler." In exchange for the Kirtland's warbler skins, Grinnell offered the skins of Townsend's warblers, hermit warblers, black-throated gray warblers and others.

Soon Wood was receiving letters from collectors and dealers all over the United States. One collector, Charles A. Allen of San Geronimo, California, enclosed a price list in his letter for bird skins he had in stock; the prices ranged from $.25 for various warblers, wrens, and tits to $1.50 for a "western red-tailed hawk" and $2.50 for a "California pigmy owl."

At Wood's request, Jim Parmalee, a resident of the area near where Wood found the nesting colony, collected a nest with eggs—not young birds—in 1904, and had them shipped to the American Museum of Natural History in New York City. But while Wood and Parmalee were collecting adults, nestlings, and eggs for science, collectors and profiteers were also descending on Oscoda County, and people living near the colony were taking eggs and selling them to collectors for as much as twenty-five dollars each.[10] A horrified editorial in the September 1904 issue of the *Bulletin of the Michigan Ornithological Club*, signed by associate editor Walter B. Barrows, lamented the impact bird collectors were having on the nesting colony and admitted that perhaps Wood's article had been too specific about the location of the colony.

The announcement in a former number of this journal of the discovery of the nesting ground of the Kirtland's Warbler created something of a sensation in ornithological circles. As might have been foreseen more than one collector planned to raid Oscoda County this summer and secure specimens of the coveted bird and its eggs. Reports of such intentions were current before the winter's snows had left the Au Sable region and many a bird-lover's blood grew hot at the thought of the certain persecution and possible extermination of the only known colony of this rare species.

Knowledge of the impending danger reached the State Game Warden too late to forestall all attempts but with his customary promptness and energy he took in the situation and made a strong effort to protect the birds. About the 20th of June every permit to take birds for scientific purposes was revoked so far as this warbler was concerned, a special deputy was added to the force in the Au Sable region, and a reward was offered for the apprehension of anyone molesting Kirtland's Warbler in any way. The effect was immediate and salutary, and every true ornithologist as well as every right-minded citizen will thank Mr. Chapman for his prompt and vigorous action while regretting that it could not have taken effect at an earlier date.

We are free to admit that the Bulletin made a serious mistake in publishing the exact locality in which the birds had been found, but at the moment the interest in the discovery and the desire to give readers the fullest information on so important an event caused a temporary suspension of caution which can be readily understood. The incident has caused some unpleasant criticism, not all of which is justified. We cheerfully take our own share of blame and promise to be more discreet in the future.

. . . Definite provision should be made by law for the collection of eggs for strictly scientific purposes and then the ordinary collector who is robbing for pleasure or especially for profit should be summarily put out of business.[11]

Wood soon found his article on the Kirtland's warbler's nesting ground in great demand and had a pamphlet of the article printed. He distributed the pamphlet to museums and ornithological societies across North America and even sent one unsolicited to the nation's bird-watcher in chief, President Theodore Roosevelt. Wood included the response in a scrapbook of letters that is stored in the Range Room of the University of Michigan Museum of Natural History.

White House.
Washington.

May 31, 1904
My dear Sir:

The pamphlet you have been good enough to forward to the President has been received, and he wishes me to thank you for your courtesy.

Very truly yours,
Secretary to the President.

Following in the steps of Wood was a "socially awkward" young man from Chicago by the name of Nathan F. Leopold Jr.[12] An accomplished ornithologist by the time he was sixteen, Leopold would be considered the world's foremost expert on the Kirtland's warbler before his nineteenth birthday.

Leopold was nothing short of a genius, as his IQ was estimated to be more than 200. In 1916, just a few days before his thirteenth birthday, he was elected to membership in the American Ornithologists' Union. In his teens, Leopold was in eager pursuit of rare birds in the Chicago area.[13] At age sixteen, his fieldwork garnered him a brief article, "Rare and Unusual Birds in the Chicago Area during the Spring of 1920," in the *Auk*.[14] By this time Leopold was already an expert ornithologist and a member of the Wilson Ornithological Society. He also taught bird study classes to wealthy elderly ladies on Chicago's South Side and spent hundreds of hours in the field, specifically in the swamps of northwestern Indiana and near the northern Michigan summer estate of his friend Richard Loeb.

Both Leopold and Loeb came from wealthy families. Both were extraordinarily smart, and both started college at the University of Chicago at the tender age of fifteen. Both transferred to the University of Michigan, but their paths diverged when Leopold transferred back to Chicago after Loeb was accepted into an Ann Arbor fraternity on one condition: Loeb must reject his friendship with Leopold because fraternity members believed Leopold was a homosexual. Angered by Loeb's rejection, Leopold transferred back to the University of Chicago, where he graduated Phi Beta Kappa. Loeb, meanwhile, graduated from the University of Michigan at age seventeen and is thought to be the school's youngest graduate ever.[15]

Before leaving Michigan, however, Leopold's life was changed when he studied birds and worked under the tutelage of Norman Wood at the University Museum. Seeing promise in his young apprentice, Wood urged Leopold to go north to study the Kirtland's warbler.[16]

On June 24, 1922, Leopold set out from Chicago with James Watson to seek the Kirtland's warbler and further establish himself in ornithological circles. (James Watson, coincidentally, was the father of James Dewey Watson, who along with Francis Crick and Maurice

Wilkins, received a Nobel Prize in 1962 for their discovery of the structure of DNA.) Similar to Wood's account of finding the first Kirtland's warbler nest, Leopold's description of his trip is part travelogue and part scientific paper. After four days of travel, Leopold and Watson arrived in northern Michigan only to discover that they had made a critical error in planning their trip: they had gone to the same location where Wood found his first Kirtland's warbler nest nearly twenty years earlier.

> [W]e saw no sign of the bird either then nor during our entire stay. The reason for this failure may be looked for chiefly in the change in the character of the country which had taken place since Mr. Wood's expedition. One of the peculiarities of *Dendroica kirtlandi* as we afterwards learned, is that it nests entirely in jack pine from five to twelve feet in height. Consequently, the very trees which twenty years before, at the time of Mr. Wood's expedition, had offered ideal nesting sites for the Warbler, had by the time of our arrival attained a much greater height, and were no longer a likely home for the bird.[17]

The lack of success did not deter Leopold. He retreated to Chicago to research the locations of other Kirtland's warbler colonies and immediately set about making plans for his return.

On June 16, 1923, Leopold left Chicago with Watson, Sydney Stein Jr., and Henry B. Steele Jr. Two days later, the four were in the field, northwest of Oscoda, Michigan.

> According to the instruction which Mr. Wood was kind enough to furnish, we started off at 12:30 P.M. to drive to Foote Dam on the Au Sable River and about seven miles from the lodge. We drove north about three quarters of a mile on M-10, the state trunk line, and then turned due west over a little sand road leading to Foote Dam. Hardly had we driven 500 yards on this road when Mr. Stein called our attention to a song which was unfamiliar to all of us, and we got out of the car to investigate. We fought our way several hundred yards through extremely dense jack-pine when Mr. Watson

and the writer simultaneously caught a view of the singer perched in a large pine tree. The bird turned out to be a fine adult male *D. kirtlandi* in full nuptial plumage. Perhaps the most striking feature of the song was its great carrying quality. The bird perches on a limb, every muscle in his body tense, points his head toward the sky and lets out a burst of clear, bubbling song, easily audible at a distance of a quarter mile. In singing, so much effort and vigor are put forth that the tension of the jugulum and throat is very noticeable and it seems as though the singer's throat will burst from the sheer force of the song.

After watching this male for twenty minutes, the four set out to try to determine the dimensions of the colony and then retired for the night.

The next day, June 19, Leopold and his companions returned to the colony and took turns observing and recording the comings and goings of the adults.

> Arrived at nest at 9:45 A.M. After difficulty in discovering nest, flushed male from its side. He flew about four feet to a small jack-pine and eyed us suspiciously for a moment—then burst into song. Moved closer to nest, with a bug in his mouth, watching us and singing. Female sat on a bush at a distance of 15 feet, chipping and wagging her tail. Male seemed at ease—the female not at all. Male sang—
> chip, chip, — chip, chip, chip, — chip, chip wheeou . . .
> 9:50—Male moved nearer nest, singing six times a minute. Head always raised in song. Movement of throat very noticeable. Female flew nearer into same clump. Food held tenaciously in mouth of male for fifteen minutes during song.
> 9:57—Male fed young. The young birds have not made a noise.
> 10:06—Male hopped from nest, looked about an instant and commenced singing.
> 10:09—Male left clump (in search of food), and flew to a neighboring tree at a distance of thirty feet, where he sang.
> 10:13—Male reentered clump with food, singing. Approached nest as before and fed.

10:14—Seems much less shy. This time stayed only 45 seconds
before reappearing, having disposed of his food. As before,
remained in clump singing for several minutes before departing in search of food. Female chipping much more softly and
much less frequently. Seems to have become accustomed to
our presence.

Female wags her tail much more frequently than male.

10:24—Male approached within two feet. Not at all suspicious
singing. Has two alarm notes, one slightly softer than the
other. Female approached within a foot of the nest and then
withdrew, wagging tail continually. Also circles around watching us very intently.

10:29—Female within six inches of nest, with food.

10:33—Male in bush to right of us, singing. Female keeps coming
within six inches of nest, withdrawing each time. She wags her
tail much more than male.

10:38—Male enters nest. Immediately leaves. Female also enters
after watching male. Also leaves immediately.

10:41—Female enters nest. She has been within six inches of the
nest twenty-eight times before entering for the first time.

(Relieved by Messrs. Steele and Stein.)

The four watched the nest until about noon, when they decided
to retire for a meal. In Oscoda, they had a chance meeting with Conservation Officer James McGillivray, who was at the time assigned
to the Conservation Department's motion picture studio.[18] McGillivray wanted to record the activities at a Kirtland's nest in the form
of a motion picture, so the five struck a deal: McGillivray would help
Leopold and his friends if they could find him a nest to photograph.
Instead of going back to the nest they had studied that morning, Leopold and his friends decided to find a new nest, one closer to a road to
make it easier for them to bring in a bulky motion picture camera and
any additional gear.

Crawling on our hands and knees we approached within a foot of
the tree. The female finally flushed from the site of the nest but
stayed so close to us that she might easily have been caught alive in

the hand by any of us. In fact, during the whole afternoon neither parent ever went further than four or five feet from the nest, chipping incessantly. . . .

The nest contained two fledglings, one very small with eyes closed, the other much larger and with eyes opened. The latter we later ascertained to be a Cowbird. After marking the tree, we retired in order not to disturb the family. In this case as in the other, the nest was very close to one of the sand roads which crisscrossed through the jack-pine.[19]

The following morning, Leopold and his party returned to the site of the second nest with McGillivray and set about preparing to record the Kirtland's warbler on film.

It was necessary to remove two small jack-pines and sundry other small foliage in order to permit the sunlight to enter the nest. We found beside the two nestlings one large speckled egg, probably a Cowbird egg. The birds were surprisingly tame, not even particularly disturbed by the sawing of trees, clearing of the site in general, or by the setting and leveling of the motion picture machine. We spent the entire morning taking pictures of the young ones and parents feeding. As in the previous case, the female was very timid, feeding only once in two-and-a-half hours. By one o'clock, we decided to remove the young Cowbird as it was getting all the food and crowding the young Kirtland's.

After lunch, in Oscoda, the five returned to the nest to film again. Upon arrival, however, they noticed something was different.

On our return at about one-thirty, there was no sign of the parents for the first half hour. Finally the male approached, singing, but made no attempt to feed. He seemed, however, to be quite at ease. Being a little alarmed at the lack of attention of the parent, we decided to take matters in our own hands and feed the young bird ourselves. Consequently, we caught several of the large horse-flies which, unfortunately, are extremely abundant. Taking one of these in my right hand and lying down on my side at the nest, I succeeded in feeding the nestling two flies very much to his satisfaction. During this operation the adult male approached very near me and scrutinized me carefully, apparently not alarmed as indicated by the infrequent twitching of his tail. . . .

At Mr. McGillivray's suggestion I lay very still and extended a fly held between the fingers of my left hand slowly toward the bird. To my great surprise after about two or three approaches and withdrawals, the bird perched on a twig within a few inches of my hand and snatched the fly, which he ate. I lay very still, and after a short time the bird became quite accustomed to me. Apparently he took this as an easy way of securing food, for he ate in all seventeen flies in this manner. Even more, he perched on my shoe, once on my thigh and again on the tip of my shoe. Mr. McGillivray meantime was attempting to photograph the proceedings and took in all twelve exposures of the incident. . . .

The male rapidly learned to perch on a particular dead twig when coming for his flies, and soon appeared irritated when we were unable to supply flies fast enough. He appeared to have an insatiable appetite.[20]

Leopold's fourteen-page article in the *Auk* concluded with a brief commentary on the cowbird.

It has long been a subject of speculation why the Kirtland's Warbler which raises as large a brood as most other Warblers, and which apparently has no more natural enemies than the other Warblers, should continue to be so extremely scarce. I suggest as a reason for this the fact that the bird is largely preyed upon by the Cowbirds (*Molothrus ater*). Wherever we saw a singing male Kirtland's there were a number of Cowbirds perched about in the tall dead trees, apparently in quest of the same thing for which we were looking. I am afraid that our first nest represented the exception, and the second where there was but one baby Kirtland, a baby Cowbird and a Cowbird's egg, the rule. It seems that the Cowbird had disposed of three or four baby Kirtland's which must have been in the nest originally. This seems the most plausible explanation.

According to comparative estimates made by Mr. Wood last year, and ourselves this year, the bird is decreasing in numbers. It is greatly to be feared that *Dendroica kirtlandi* may soon be another of the American birds on the extinct list.

Leopold's experience in the jack pine woods would take him to another place, specifically, the annual meeting of the American Ornithologists' Union in Cambridge, Massachusetts. On the final day of the 1923 meeting, Leopold presented the motion picture made by McGillivray and discussed his findings at the nest.[21]

Besides being a promising ornithologist, Leopold was a fan of the philosopher Friedrich Nietzsche, whose writings criticizing morality and Christianity were popular on college campuses during the early twentieth century. Influenced by Nietzsche's writing, Leopold considered himself a superman who possessed superior qualities that transcended human characteristics. Anyone who possessed those characteristics, Nietzsche wrote and Leopold believed, was not bound to obey the moral codes that controlled the actions of other, less superior people. After committing a series of petty crimes without being suspected, Leopold and his former classmate, Loeb, decided it was time to increase the thrill. To really prove themselves Nietzschean supermen, they would commit the perfect murder.

On May 21, 1924, Leopold and Loeb lured a neighbor boy, Bobby Franks, into a car, where they struck him on the head with a chisel and stuffed a rag in his mouth. Within an hour, Franks was dead. To prove their superior qualities, Leopold and Loeb drove around for an hour with Franks's lifeless body in the backseat of the car. After visiting a drive-in restaurant, they drove to a spot Leopold knew well from birding—Wolf Lake in Hammond, Indiana. At Wolf Lake, they stripped Franks of his clothes and poured acid onto his face to make identification more difficult. They then stuffed the body into a culvert, and went home to write a ransom note. It was the perfect murder—or so they thought. While disposing of Franks, Leopold accidentally let a pair of glasses slip from his pocket. The glasses had an unusual hinge, and a Chicago optometrist told police that only three pairs had been sold in the entire city. The optometrist provided detectives with a list of names. One of the names was Nathan Leopold's.

Chicago, at that time, was in the midst of a brutal crime wave that the police seemed unable to deal with it. The city's newspapers cried out for justice while simultaneously trying to outdo the competition by sensationalizing each new crime. After the arrest of Leopold and Loeb, the papers portrayed them as two bored intellectuals who had murdered a young boy for the thrill of it.

Loeb's family hired attorney Clarence Darrow, already famous as a criminal defense attorney for representing union leader Eugene V. Debs during the Pullman strike of 1894. Darrow was an ardent opponent of capital punishment. He immediately recognized that Leopold and Loeb were in danger of being sent to the gallows and urged them to take a gamble: They could risk a jury trial, which would give the prosecution two chances to achieve a guilty sentence on charges that automatically received the death penalty, or they could plead guilty and ask to be sentenced by a judge who might—might!—merely sentence them to life in prison.

Darrow's closing statement is legendary. In a twelve-hour hearing, Darrow leaned heavily on the humanity of the judge. He argued that Leopold and Loeb were not fully responsible for their actions because of their upbringing and youth. He suggested that an eye-for-an-eye system of punishment harked back to the laws of the jungle and was not fit for a modern state. He asked the judge if he could, in good conscience, send two nineteen-year-old boys to their deaths. When Darrow was finished, there were tears on the face of the judge and the courtroom sat in stunned silence. Darrow's gamble worked; Leopold and Loeb received life sentences for the murder plus ninety-nine years for the kidnapping.

Prison life was a difficult adjustment for Leopold, but he found ways to keep intellectually busy. He worked in the prison library and reorganized the collection with a modern classification system after it was trashed in a prison riot. He taught fellow inmates to read. He established a school that taught English grammar, foreign languages, and mathematics from basic arithmetic to trigonometry. When not teaching others, Leopold also taught himself twenty-seven foreign languages, operated an X-ray machine in the prison infirmary, and helped to organize prisoners in a World War II study on an experimental malaria vaccination for soldiers fighting in the Pacific.

Despite living in a windowless prison cell, Leopold's memoir, *Life Plus 99 Years,* makes it clear that birds were never far from his thoughts, and he cherished the robin and horned lark he briefly had as pets in his cell. Although prison life was boring, there were occasional breaks that brought Leopold great joy. One of those times came a few years into his imprisonment, when he received a visit from an old friend.

A year before my arrest I had collected, in Michigan, some specimens of an extremely rare bird, the Kirtland's warbler. I had brought back home one whole family group of the birds, the two adults and the nest, containing two nestling Kirtland's warblers, a nestling cowbird, and a cowbird egg. The cowbird, which builds no nest of its own, parasitizes other birds by laying its eggs in their nests and is, I think, a major cause of the extreme rarity of the Kirtland's warbler. I had collected the nest in its natural setting and brought back a piece of the ground, about three feet square, on which the nest was located. It contained much underbrush and a jack-pine tree about four feet high. I had entrusted the work of preparing the habitat group to one of the leading taxidermists in the city, Mr. Ashley Hine of the Field Museum. Since he had to work on my group in his leisure time and since the work entailed removing, waxing, painting, and replacing each individual pine needle and each blade of grass, the work occupied him nearly two years. Finally in the summer of 1925, it was ready. I wanted to give the group to the Field Museum, for only one other group exists in the world, but I wanted awfully to see it first. Warden Whitman was most gracious about granting permission, and one day Sven, the chauffeur who had been with our family since I was six months old, bought the large case down to the prison. I was called to the warden's office and permitted to admire it for half an hour.[22]

After thirty-three years in prison, Nathan Leopold's sentence was commuted. To avoid publicity, he immediately moved to Puerto Rico to teach mathematics and work in a local hospital as an X-ray technician. With his new freedom, Leopold's thoughts returned to birds. Noticing that there was little information about the birds of his new home, he authored *Checklist of birds of Puerto Rico and the Virgin Islands.*[23] Leopold also married, made several close friends, and set about reviving his relationship with his longtime special friend, the Kirtland's warbler.

Shortly before being released from prison, Leopold began corresponding with Douglas Middleton, a Detroit Audubon Society member, citizen scientist, and participant in the first Kirtland's warbler census in 1951. Middleton initially wrote to Leopold to request permission to reprint Leopold's article "The Kirtland's Warbler in Its Summer Home" in the *Auk*. Leopold gladly granted permission and, in return asked Middleton if he would help two of his friends find the Kirtland's warbler during an upcoming visit to Michigan. The requests would launch a friendship with the warbler as the linchpin. Leopold not only granted Middleton permission but also offered assistance to Harold Mayfield, who was in the process of writing a definitive book on the Kirtland's warbler.

> It does occur to me that I have in storage in the States the original motion picture of the Kirtland's Warbler at its nesting sight [*sic*] (Oscoda in this case) which we made in June 1923 and which I showed at the meeting of the A.O.U. in Cambridge, Mass., in October of that year. It has been stored these 35 years in a conventional lead motion-picture container and I have no idea whether it would still be usable. . . . Further, the photography is that of 1923 and anything but expert. But if this monograph is to contain certain historical sections concerning what has been known about Kirtland's at various times, perhaps the film might be of some use to you or Mr Mayfield. If you think it would be of any value, I should be glad to arrange to have it sent to you. I also still retain title to the habitat group of Kirtland's with nest and nestlings, which is now stored at the Museum of Natural Science [the facility now known the Field Museum] in Chicago. This might be somewhat more dif-

ficult to get hold of, but that too might perhaps be done if it would
be of any use in the proposed monograph.[24]

Leopold and Middleton would continue to correspond, and the
two ended up visiting Kirtland's warbler country together.

> Dear Doug,
> I am heartily ashamed to note, on consulting my file to get your
> street address, that I apparently haven't written you in almost two
> years—since my return from my vacation in the States in July
> 1964, which included meeting you personally and our memorable
> trip to the Au Sable country. . . .
>   Altho I am not yet quite sure, the way it looks now is that I can
> and *must* take my vacation after working hours of June 28. Sup-
> pose I got a plane that late afternoon or evening and came directly
> to Detroit. (1) Would it be possible for you to go up to the K.W.
> territory with me then? (2) Would it be too late to hope to catch
> the birds still in song?

Leopold not only made it to Michigan, but he was escorted into the
jack pine by Bill Irvine, a young U.S. Forest Service wildlife biologist.
Irvine remembers being called in to the office by the district ranger
and introduced to Leopold. Irvine said that at the time of the introduction Leopold's name rang a bell, but it wasn't until the two were in a
car, several miles out of town, that the bell turned into a claxon. "We
were driving down the road," he said, "and he was just sitting there. I
looked over at him and said to myself, 'Now I know who you are.'" He
glanced out of the corner of his eyes and recoiled as he remembered
the incident.

On a June 1964 visit to Michigan, Leopold took a side trip to visit
his Kirtland's display at the Field Museum in Chicago and tell curators that he wished to have the display moved to a different museum
after his death. Shortly after returning to Puerto Rico, he decided he
wouldn't wait and ordered the transfer of his Kirtland's group from
the Field Museum to the Cranbrook Institute of Science, a natural his-

tory museum in suburban Detroit. Shortly after Leopold decided to make the switch, he wrote to Middleton.

> I should like to add, Doug, that ever since I sent the group to Cran-brook I've felt really good about it every time I've thought of it. That is obviously the proper place for it, and making the ante-mortem gift was certainly the wise thing to do. I am most grateful to you for making the suggestion when I asked your opinion. The only thing I regret is that you were overly modest in your article and did not mention that I chose Cranbrook at your suggestion. I knew of Cranbrook only as a name, appearing as publisher of Mayfield's book, and didn't even know that it was a museum. But for you, I should certainly never have thought of it, and the group would likely have wound up in the Smithsonian Institution or the New York Museum of Natural History. Both middling fair institu-tions, but not to be compared with Cranbrook, for *they* don't have a Kirtland's group![25]

Despite Leopold's character flaw, which allowed Nietzsche to have such a profound and warped influence, it's clear that his thoughts on the Kirtland's warbler have withstood the test of time. Looking back at his "The Kirtland's Warbler in Its Summer Home," a reader cannot help but be struck by the accuracy of his observations, particularly when it came to one of the biggest threats posed to the Kirtland's warbler.

TWO : An Amazing Set of Pipes

Nearly everyone who has encountered a male Kirtland's warbler singing on his territory has come away with the same opinion: He's absolutely charming.

Casual birders are wowed at the sight of a male Kirtland's sitting on the top of a tree surveying his territory and advertising himself to potential mates. Even researchers, who claim to be objective in the pursuit of science, describe the warbler's low-pitched song as "cheery," "joyous," and "lively." They also agree that the six-inch-long bird has something in common with the greatest operatic tenors: they can both belt it out.

A male Kirtland's warbler is a vigorous singer. If the weather is right, he will sing between 5 and 9 times a minute during the early morning hours.[1] Harold Mayfield documented one male singing 165 times between 5:16 and 6:30 a.m. on an early June morning when the temperature was below freezing.[2] On a late June day in 1956, he heard a male singing 2,212 times between 5 a.m. and 8 p.m.[3]

The warbler's effort also results in an unusually loud song.

"Perhaps the most striking feature of the song was its great carrying quality," Nathan Leopold Jr. wrote in 1924. "In singing, so much effort and vigor are put forth that the tension of the jugulum and throat is very noticeable and it seems as though the singer's throat will burst from the sheer force of the song."[4]

One thing that nobody seems to agree on, however, is what exactly the Kirtland's warbler song sounds like. Some people say it bubbles like that of a house wren. Others say it whistles like a that of a Baltimore oriole. Still others have compared it to the song of the northern waterthrush or yellow-throated warbler. Researchers and writers who have tried to describe the Kirtland's warbler's song in human syllables have ended up with jaw-droppingly different interpretations.

After discovering the Kirtland's warbler's nesting grounds in northern Michigan in 1903, Norman Wood wrote, "This song may be described as follows: *weche chee-chee-chee-chee-r-r-r.* The 'r' sound is quite prolonged and loud. The first two notes are low, then the notes gradually increase in volume to the end."[5]

A year after Wood's discovery of the breeding ground, Edward Arnold of Battle Creek, Michigan, described the male's song as: "*Trp, trp, terp, terp, terp, ser-wit, er, wer,* all but the first two notes uttered rapidly."[6]

Leopold in 1924 described the song as "*chip, chip, —— chip, chip, chip, —— chip, chip wheeou.*"[7]

So, how does *weche chee-chee-chee-chee-r-r-r* become *Trp, trp, terp, terp, terp, ser-wit, er, wer* or *chip, chip, —— chip, chip, chip, —— chip, chip wheeou*? Are we talking about the same bird?

Thankfully, Harold Axtell came along in 1938 to sort things out. Axtell was part of a team of Cornell University researchers that filmed singing Kirtland's warblers for study. The problem with the Kirtland's warbler's song, Axtell wrote, is that there is so much going on at once that it's impossible for the human ear to sort it all out. And, given that one person's ears may be considerably more perceptive than another's or that one individual may have lost some acuity with age, "Probably only a person who has himself heard and tried to select the best (if any!) possible syllabication for the sound can appreciate how *weet weet* and *r-r* may possibly both refer to the same sound."[8]

Carefully listening to several different male Kirtland's warblers sing, Axtell detected several different syllabications and uses a method of graphically transcribing birdsong developed by Aretas A. Saunders in *A Guide to Bird Songs* in 1935.

Chu chu chi chi *chi-oo-wi-oo*
Chert chert chert cher *chi chi-oo-wi-wi*

Chu chu   chu chu che che wi-oo-wi-oo

Kler   Kler Kler Kler che che chu chu chu

He concluded:

> So with these individual differences in our hearing, we may in an extreme instance have two people listening to the same warbler song, each hearing it with equal intensity, but with one hearing four notes, the other hearing twelve. Neither of them can hear what the bird actually does with its voice. As revealed by a study of the film recording, a Kirtland's Warbler may sing more than a hundred notes in a second, most of which follow one another too rapidly for any human ear to distinguish. To make matters worse, the quality may sound to one of the listeners like that of an oriole, to the other like that of a Yellowthroated Warbler, whereas to a more "average" listener, it will sound like neither. Then there is the simple psychological factor of suggestion or first association by which we hear a bird song for the first time and are immediately impressed with how much it reminds us of this or that bird, and thereafter, because of this initial prejudice, we cannot understand how other people can say that it sounds more like something still different. . . . The Kirtland's Warbler as a species does not have just one song of so many notes and a certain syllabication, nor does it have just two such songs, nor is it limited to several distinct songs. Not only does an individual sing differently from any of his neighbors, but he changes his own song several times each day. Even while singing essentially the same song, a little perhaps accidental variation is indulged in now and then, such as the omission or interjection of one or two notes, slurring a couple of notes usually sung separately, variations in relative pitch of one or two notes, and a gradual shifting in key of the song as a whole through a range of nearly three tones. Most of these minor variations would not be twice repeated in the same way, but are apparently unintentional when they occur. Occasionally, however, they would constitute a new variation which the singer would retain for a time. More commonly these more enduring revisions would involve a sudden shift

in pitch or in rhythm or both of an entire group of notes in the song. Then this would be repeated several times or through several singing periods, in some cases for several hours. It was my observation that when a new variation was selected for its share of repetition, the previous song was not again used.[9]

It may seem as if Axtell's exhaustive effort would be the definitive word, but in 1960 Harold Mayfield jumped in and compared the Kirtland's song to a well-known Glenn Miller tune: "I suggest that the staccato tones, emphatic nature, and duration of the typical song may be roughly conveyed through the title of an erstwhile popular song: 'ch-ch-chatanooga-choo-choo' uttered rapidly, with a slurring start, a drop in pitch, and a double note at the close."[10]

Although the wide variation in song may make it more difficult for the casual birder to recognize a Kirtland's warbler in the field, it's actually helpful to researchers; those who work with the Kirtland's on a daily basis are able to recognize individual males just by the sound of their songs. Lawrence Walkinshaw, who spent fifty years doing fieldwork on the Kirtland's warbler from the 1930s through the 1980s, always knew when he was near one particular bird he had nicknamed "Mr. Odd Song."[11] And Sarah Rockwell, a doctoral student at the University of Maryland who actively bands Kirtland's warblers and is conducting a five-year field study to determine whether the quality of the winter habitat in the Bahamas has any impact on nesting success in Michigan, says she is familiar with two males that have songs resembling a horse's whinny—a descending *choo-choo wee-wee-wee-wee.*

But there's more to the Kirtland's warbler's song than merely vocalization—this bird rocks. In song, the Kirtland's warbler has stage presence, and he's like Bruce Springsteen in his intensity and effort.

"In song every muscle in the bird's body seems to be tense, the head and neck are stretched upward pointing almost directly to the sky, the tail is stretched down and the whole body inclined forward," Leopold wrote. "So vigorous is the song that the expansion and contraction of the throat are noticeable even from some distance. The bill is open wide, it being remarkable that food can be retained therein during song."[12]

In most homes singing with one's mouth full would be considered poor table manners, but Rockwell is thankful for this bad etiquette. When she hears a male slurring his song, she knows that he is likely singing with his mouth full; he's bringing a yummy caterpillar or blueberry to his mate on the nest or to their young. When she finds a male Kirtland's singing with his mouth full, she knows there is a good chance that he will lead her to his nest. Once Rockwell finds a nest, she will check it three times during the nesting season and record its progress.

Carol Bocetti, a professor at California University of Pennsylvania, has been conducting research on the Kirtland's warbler for more than twenty years. During that time she has learned subtle differences in songs. Not only can she tell males apart, but she can tell when one is communicating with a potential mate and has noticed that his song is softer and the pitch higher than when he is singing to establish his territory. Bocetti refers to this song as "sweet talking."

Here's hoping his lady finds him as charming as we humans do.

THREE : The Cowbird Cometh

What might go through a Kirtland's warbler's brain when it sees a brown-headed cowbird in the area of its nest? Does the warbler recognize the cowbird as a threat? Or does it simply look at the cowbird blankly?

The Kirtland's warbler likely had little or no contact with the cowbird between the retreat of the North American ice sheet and the start of the twentieth century. For ten thousand years, the warbler commuted between the northern Michigan pine barrens and the Bahamas, while the cowbird wandered across the Great Plains with the bison herds, never encountering one another.

Molothrus ater became known as the "cowbird" because it was often seen associating with Great Plains cattle.[1] In the nineteenth century, however, it was known as the "buffalo bird" because of its close relationship with the American bison. The cowbird traveled with the bison across the short-grass prairie in the middle of the North American continent, migrating north with the herd in spring and south with it in the fall. The cowbirds depended partially on the grazing bison for food, gleaning seeds and grains from the ground and also eating the insects swirling around the bison as they grazed. In return for helping the cowbirds find food, the bison depended on the cowbird to pluck insects off them as they rested.[2]

The symbiotic relationship with the bison helped the cowbird forge its reproductive strategy. While most bird species on the Great Plains were looking for some quiet spot in which to build a nest and raise their young safely away from predators, the cowbird could not afford

Lawrence Walkinshaw, a dentist, amateur ornithologist, and citizen scientist from Battle Creek, Michigan, was the first person to band a Kirtland's warbler. He is probably more famous for his international research on cranes, but his fieldwork in Michigan resulted in a statistical analysis of the Kirtland's warbler nesting success rate that demonstrated the impact of predations by the brown-headed cowbird. Walkinshaw is pictured here in Sweden. (Courtesy of the Bentley Historical Library, University of Michigan.)

to go on maternity leave. With the bison constantly on the move— twenty miles or more a day—the cowbird needed some way to have its young and keep up with the herd at the same time. The cowbird developed a simple but brilliant strategy: lay an egg in another bird's nest and move on. That strategy, known by ornithologists as "brood parasitism," has served the cowbird well. A female cowbird can lay more than thirty eggs in one season, and cowbird eggs have been documented in the nests of more than 220 different North American bird species.[3]

To disguise its visit, a female cowbird will often remove an egg from the host bird's nest when it lays its own egg. To further help its abandoned offspring, the cowbird often will return to a nest a few days later and remove another of the host bird's eggs.[4]

If a potential host bird fails to recognize a cowbird egg in its nest it puts its own offspring at risk. The incubation period for a cowbird egg is shorter than those of most other birds (ten to twelve versus twelve to fourteen days), which allows the cowbird egg to hatch before or concurrently with the host bird's eggs. Because the female cowbird mostly lays its eggs in the nests of smaller songbirds, a newly hatched cowbird likely will be larger than the host bird's young. Lawrence Walkinshaw, one of the giants of Kirtland's warbler research, documented the size difference between a young cowbird and two young Kirtland's warblers. In 1971, Walkinshaw found a nest in Crawford County, Michigan, containing one young cowbird and two young Kirtland's. The cowbird weighed 13.2 grams, while a one-day-old Kirtland's weighed 2.4 grams and another Kirtland's that had hatched earlier that same day weighed just 1.4 grams.[5] The cowbird's size advantage allows it to dominate its smaller and weaker nest mates, particularly at mealtime. Eventually, the bigger, stronger, and healthier cowbird will push one or more of its defenseless mates out of the nest. Any Kirtland's nest with two cowbird eggs in it is certain to fail.[6] What made it worse for the Kirtland's warbler was that so many of their nests were being parasitized. A Walkinshaw study of fifty-two nesting pairs between 1966 and 1971 showed that 69 percent of the warblers' nests had been parasitized.[7]

In his book *Nest Observations of the Kirtland's Warbler: A Half-Century Quest,* Walkinshaw expressed deep concern at what the cowbird was doing to the warbler population. In 1966, he wrote that he had visited six different Kirtland's nests in late June and early July and found that each of them contained either cowbird eggs or fledgling cowbirds and no Kirtland's young.

> Found 4 July 1966 (1 fledged cowbird) It really looks serious. This one can fly a little. In every case above I searched and watched the birds looking for fledged KWs. In no case was this found. . . . Of the 7 1966 records this was the only one successful. Between 1957 and 1966 things look very serious for the Kirtland's Warbler.[8]

By 1970, Walkinshaw was taking matters into his own hands and destroying cowbird eggs by drilling a small hole in the egg and placing it back in the nest or by destroying cowbird nestlings. Reading between the lines of the entries in Walkinshaw's field notebook, it becomes clear that he felt some satisfaction with his actions.

> 30 May 1970. . . . The nest was the usual coarse grasses outside with finer ones inside. There was some deer hair in the lining. 31 May–1 June the nest was completed. We were gone then until 15 June. Now the nest contained 3 KW eggs and 2 C eggs (the latter were removed). . . . This nest would have failed had we not removed the Cowbird eggs. As it was, it probably brought off 3 fledged Kirtland's Warblers.[9]

Walkinshaw was born in 1904 and raised on a farm in Calhoun County near what is now a Michigan Audubon Society sanctuary. At age five, he saw a stuffed sandhill crane in the parlor of a neighbor's house and was infatuated. As an older child, he started a junior Audubon club in his one-room schoolhouse and often ditched his farm chores to watch birds. At Olivet College, a biology professor told Walkinshaw that there was no money in ornithology, so he transferred to the University of Michigan for dentistry; it became a vocation that would give him enough flexibility and money to continue to study birds in his spare time.

Perhaps no other amateur birder has accomplished more in his or her spare time than Walkinshaw. When not seeing patients, he:

> helped to save three endangered species, the Kirtland's warbler, the whooping crane, and the sandhill crane
> served as president of the Michigan Audubon Society
> led the effort to establish the world's first crane sanctuary
> led the fight to outlaw crane hunting and end the bounty on the northern harrier
> studied and wrote extensively about fourteen of the world's fifteen crane species. The only crane species Walkinshaw did not study was the Siberian crane of Central Asia because the Soviet Union would not allow him to enter the country during the cold war era.

By the time Walkinshaw died in 1993, he had helped to establish six bird sanctuaries around the world, including one in the demilitarized zone between North and South Korea, and had written two books on the Kirtland's warbler and sixty books on cranes. His work on crane preservation was featured in *Life* magazine in 1954, with photographs of Walkinshaw taken by the renowned Alfred Eisenstadt. Today Walkinshaw is considered the father of crane research.

Walkinshaw had boundless energy; he would often wake up well before dawn to go birding, start seeing patients at 8:00 a.m., and work until 5:30 or later if needed. As leader of a local Boy Scout troop, he helped to instill a love of the outdoors in several of the kids. One of the scouts, Wayne Tice, remembers going birding regularly with Walkinshaw before school during the spring. After Tice arrived at school tardy a couple of times, the principal called Tice into his office for a good scolding. A few days later, the principal called Tice into his office again. This time he was told he could be tardy as often as he wanted as long as he was out birding with "Doc Walkinshaw."

Walkinshaw was a large, imposing man. Everyone who knew him described him as a complete gentleman and a gentle man. Even though he had beefy hands, his dental training gave him the skill to handle birds deftly and the dexterity to feed a fly or a blueberry to a female sitting on a nest. In 1932, Walkinshaw became the first person to band a Kirtland's warbler. He told Andrew Berger, another ornithologist interested in the Kirtland's warbler, that the female he had banded was so tame that he simply reached out and picked her off a branch.[10] Not only did Walkinshaw band this female, but he photographed her perched on his hand. When he checked the nest, which he did daily for a week, the female would land on his shoulder or arm or on a branch inches away. So Walkinshaw put his camera on a tripod, tied a string to the shutter release, and took a photo of her sitting on his free hand.

Starting in the late 1950s, Walkinshaw was the only person the U.S. Fish and Wildlife Service would allow to handle a Kirtland's warbler. The agency gave him the job in part because he was better than anyone else at finding a warbler's nest. That ability stemmed from his tremendous patience; his fellow field workers would often see him sit motionless for long periods observing the warblers' movements, despite being bitten by blackflies so many times that blood trickled down his face.

When in the field, Walkinshaw would often sleep in his station wagon parked near the Kirtland's warbler colony he was planning to visit that day. When he was able to visit a Kirtland's nest multiple times in the same season, he would track its progress by carefully using a pencil to write a number on each egg in the order it was laid. He would then closely follow the progress of the nest, weighing and measuring each bird as it grew. Following a nest in this way, Walkinshaw could anticipate when the birds would be old enough to fledge and leave. A day or two before fledging, he would return and band the nestlings. He often banded the adults, too. In one case he actually reached into a nest and lifted a female off the eggs to weigh, measure, and band her.[11]

The year 1931 proved to be a particularly important one for Walkinshaw; he traveled north to see his first Kirtland's warbler and begin nearly fifty years of fieldwork. He also met the woman who later became his wife. Jerry Weinrich, a retired endangered species biologist for the Michigan Department of Natural Resources, says that Walkinshaw and his wife, Clara, spent their honeymoon in a tent in northern Michigan so he could be up early to work on his Kirtland's study.

"She was just a peach," Weinrich says with some amazement.

If the cowbird is so dastardly and so easily able to invade the unoccupied nests of other bird species, what keeps it from taking over the world? Thankfully, nature has a way of finding a balance. Some bird species that have had long-term contact with the cowbird have developed defenses. The yellow warbler, for example, has learned to recognize a cowbird's egg and will abandon any nest in which it finds one. The yellow warbler's strategy is to build a new nest on top of the old one. Unfortunately, the cowbird is equally persistent. There have been documented reports of yellow warblers building six-tiered nests in response to repeated cowbird nest parasitism.[12] The gray catbird has learned to recognize the cowbird's eggs because, Harold Mayfield believed, the catbird's "deep-green egg contrasts sharply with the pale speckled egg of the cowbird," and the catbird "promptly throws out the offending object."[13] Other species have improved their reproductive odds by having two broods. Because the cowbird lays its eggs early in the nesting season, the odds of cowbird nest parasitism decline considerably for any species attempting a second brood later in the nesting season.

In the Kirtland's warbler, however, the cowbird seems to have found a complete dupe. Although there have been anecdotal reports of Kirtland's warblers abandoning their nests or removing cowbird eggs,[14] there is no proof that the warbler's actions were intentional. Furthermore, the bond between a Kirtland's warbler parent and a cowbird fledgling seems strong—at least on the warbler's side. Mike DeCapita, a field biologist with the U.S. Fish and Wildlife Service, said that, although it happened only once, he and other employees watched an adult Kirtland's warbler pass through the one-inch mesh chicken wire surrounding a cowbird trap to feed a cowbird fledgling inside, then depart the same way. DeCapita said that they allowed the warbler to feed the fledgling a few times so they could watch the behavior, then they decided to dispatch the cowbird fledgling to discourage the warbler from continuing.

And the relationship between the Kirtland's warbler and the cowbird may even be more complex than a Joan Crawford–type bird taking advantage of Ozzie and Harriet. In 1961, Harold Mayfield watched a female cowbird as it watched a female Kirtland's warbler build a nest. Mayfield began to wonder if there was something more to the cowbird's interest than simply seeking a location in which to dump an egg.

> The cowbird's interest in the nest of the Kirtland's Warbler, as has been noted with other host species, first becomes apparent during nest building. At this time the female cowbird sits on an exposed perch some distance away and watches for extended periods while the warbler works. The span of attention of the cowbird is far longer than would be required merely to locate the nest. In a higher animal we might interpret this behavior as vicarious participation, and the term may not be totally amiss here. Certainly, the cowbird's involvement would seem to be deeper than that of a mere onlooker, if it is brought to ovulation as a result of this experience.[15]

Mayfield also noticed that female cowbirds were cunning in their approach.

> Doubtless, most of the cowbird's attention to nests centers in the building and egg-laying periods—that is, before incubation begins. At these times the cowbird is not likely to be opposed by the hosts, since small songbirds typically spend a very small part of these days near the nest. Also such cowbird visits are not likely to be recorded, for it is not often that a human observer will be watching a nest constantly from concealment at these stages.
>
> Cowbird visits are probably less frequent after incubation begins. Now the nest is closely defended, and the cowbird is usually routed before it gets to the nest. Further, it appears hesitant in manner and more easily repelled in these broad-daylight visits than in the predawn, egg-laying visits . . . I saw a female Kirtland's Warbler put an unresisting female cowbird to flight three times in two days when the cowbird walked up to within a meter of the nest. This nest held young birds almost ready to leave.

If humans want to help the Kirtland's warbler, why not just remove the cowbird eggs from Kirtland's warbler nests each spring? There are several problems with that strategy. First, the process of finding a Kirtland's nest is both labor intensive and time consuming. Kirtland's warbler nests are very well concealed, and even professional researchers who have spent years in the field have trouble finding them. Second, any human visit to a nest leaves a scent trail that may make it easier for a predator to find. Third, because the nest is hidden on the ground, there's always a risk that a well-intentioned human may accidentally destroy it during the search. Finally, a female Kirtland's knows how many eggs are in the nest—even if she doesn't know how many eggs she laid. That may be partially attributed to the color of the two eggs. Kirtland's warbler and cowbird eggs are similar in color and pattern. The major difference between the two appears to be size, and that difference is measured in millimeters. The similar size and coloration may make it difficult for the Kirtland's warbler to recognize an imposter.

Walkinshaw discovered that removing an unhatched cowbird egg caused a female Kirtland's to abandon the nest. Jerry Weinrich says that Walkinshaw was troubled by this dilemma. Was it better to remove a cowbird egg and risk having the female Kirtland's abandon the nest, or was it better to leave the cowbird egg in hopes that one or two of the Kirtland's might survive and fledge?

Imagine being like Lawrence Walkinshaw and getting close enough to a Kirtland's warbler that it might land on your hand, your knee, or your shoe. Or close enough that you are able to feed it a fly from your hand, as Nathan Leopold did. For many bird-watchers an interaction like that with a Kirtland's warbler would be a dream come true. Most bird species view humans as potential predators and therefore keep a suspicious distance. Venture into the northern Michigan jack pine habitat as Leopold, Walkinshaw, and Mayfield did, and a Kirtland's may just come to you.

So many researchers have had such up-close experiences with the Kirtland's warbler on its nesting grounds that it's impossible for them not to refer to the bird as tame. But why? What is it in the nature of a Kirtland's that makes it so much less guarded around humans, especially when it is nesting and its eggs and young are so vulnerable?

In his 1960 book *The Kirtland's Warbler* Mayfield speculates that the answer can be found in the warblers' summer habitat, which is inhospitable to predators and other species that would compete for the same resources.[16] Perhaps because there are so few threats, Mayfield speculated, the Kirtland's doesn't view a human as a significant threat either.

This wasn't the only time Mayfield tossed off a thought based totally on speculation. Friends say that he was unafraid of thinking out loud and was secure enough in himself that he would throw out an idea for people to chew on, even if there was a good chance that he was wrong. Perhaps the biggest leap Mayfield made was when he speculated in print in the *Wilson Bulletin* that the Kirtland's warbler had nested in the southeastern United States ten thousand years earlier, when Michigan was covered by a glacier.

It is unlikely that the warbler was a significantly different creature in the late Pleistocene. It is a well-marked species, and Charles G. Sibley (pers. comm.) has expressed the opinion from DNA-based analysis that it probably separated from closely related *Dendroica* more than 100,000 years ago. We cannot be sure it has not changed its nesting behavior and habitat during the last 10,000 years, but its present rarity argues against its adaptability.[17]

I suggest, therefore, that for a time near the end of the Pleistocene the bird's nesting range may have been restricted to the sandy coastal plain of the South Atlantic States. Similarly, other birds now breeding in the northern coniferous forest zone may have been limited to the southeastern corner of the United States by the concentration of pinelands there. This circumstance, along with the possible origin of these species in the West Indies or beyond, may help explain why their fall migration route carries them southeast toward the sea instead of south across the midcontinent toward Mexico and Central America.[18]

Of course, there was no evidence to support this idea.

Mayfield was a contemporary of Walkinshaw's, and although the two of them did similar and somewhat competing fieldwork they could easily occupy the same room. Like Walkinshaw, Mayfield was not an ornithologist; he was a businessman and semiprofessional basketball player from Toledo, Ohio, who suffered a stroke while in his late twenties. No longer able to participate in athletics, he chose a new hobby: birds. Before his death in 2007, he would pen several articles on birds for peer-reviewed journals, including a breeding study of the red phalarope. Relying on his master's degree in mathematics, Mayfield created a technique for measuring nesting success that would become known as the "Mayfield method." His article describing the technique is the most cited work in the history of the *Wilson Journal of Ornithology*. He is also the only person to have served as president of the Wilson and Cooper ornithological societies and the American Ornithologists' Union.[19] Although he never received a doctorate, Mayfield was given an appointment as an adjunct professor of biology at the University of Toledo. While much of what Walkinshaw learned about the Kirtland's

Josselyn Van Tyne became curator of birds at the University of Michigan Museum of Natural History in 1931. He was another towering figure in ornithology, serving as president of the Wilson Ornithological Society and conducting research around the world. As curator of birds, he turned the museum into a major center for ornithological research. He contributed the chapter on the Kirtland's warbler to Arthur Bent's *Life Histories of North American Wood Warblers.* He died in 1957, never writing his planned book on the Kirtland's warbler. (Courtesy of the Bird Division, University of Michigan Exhibit Museum of Natural History.)

warbler came from his own fieldwork, Mayfield learned while assisting Josselyn Van Tyne in the field starting in 1944.

Van Tyne followed Norman Wood as curator of birds at the University of Michigan Museum of Zoology and started his study of the Kirtland's warbler in 1930. Van Tyne banded his first Kirtland's warbler four days after Walkinshaw banded his first, but it's believed that at the time the two were ignorant of each other's work. Once Walkinshaw became aware of Van Tyne's fieldwork, he stepped aside for two decades to study cranes. For more than twenty years, Van Tyne was the "go-to guy" for information in the Kirtland's warbler, and he showed his knowledge by contributing a chapter on the Kirtland's warbler to Arthur Bent's *Life Histories of North American Wood Warblers,* which was published in 1953.

Van Tyne was a towering figure in both ornithology and the field.

One of the American Ornithologists' Union's top research awards is named after him; the award is given annually to provide support for research into avian biology. And, at six feet, seven inches tall, Van Tyne could be seen above the young jack pines when his normal-sized colleagues were obscured by the dense branches. Under his watch, Van Tyne turned the University of Michigan Museum of Zoology into a major center for ornithological research in North America. Among his contributions to the field was being the first to instruct students to measure and record the size and weight of each specimen's gonads. It's quite the paradox for a man who was considered by many to be organized and rigid in his behavior to the point of being prudish.

Van Tyne had planned to write a book on the Kirtland's warbler, but his pressing work at the museum, as a professor on campus, as the editor of the *Wilson Bulletin,* and as president of the American Ornithologists' Union kept him from being able to follow through. After Van Tyne's death in 1957, Mayfield continued Van Tyne's fieldwork and used his field notes to write the definitive book on the Kirtland's warbler. The book would earn Mayfield the Brewster Medal for exceptional work from the American Ornithologists' Union.

On his own, Mayfield would become a giant in the field of ornithology, and his impact on the Kirtland's warbler continues into the twenty-first century in the form of a simple task: an annual census that keeps tabs on the Kirtland's warbler population. Mayfield organized the first census in June 1951—one hundred years after Pease shot his specimen—and decided it should be held every ten years. Mayfield's idea was groundbreaking because no one had ever attempted a complete census of a single bird species before. A similar census would be pretty much impossible for just about every other North American bird species because they range over such a wide area. Counting the Kirtland's, however, would not only be feasible but relatively easy for a couple of reasons. First, the warbler's range was limited; it had never been recorded in more than twelve Michigan counties in an area that spanned eighty-five miles from north to south and one hundred from east to west. Second, there was no needle-in-the-haystack factor. The Kirtland's warbler's preference for young jack pines and sandy soil made it easy to identify potential nesting sites. Third, it would be easy

Harold Mayfield, a business executive from Toledo, Ohio, spent many years in the field studying the Kirtland's warbler with Josselyn Van Tyne. After Van Tyne's death, Mayfield wrote the definitive book on the Kirtland's warbler, using much of Van Tyne's research. Mayfield also wrote several articles on birds for ornithological journals. He is the only person to have served as president of the Wilson and Cooper ornithological societies and the American Ornithologists' Union. (Courtesy of the *Toledo Blade*.)

to count the males because their loud and steady song made them easy to locate. Last, the distinctive nature of the warblers' song made it easy to identify; there would be no reason to actually see the bird in order to be sure it was a Kirtland's.

More than thirty people participated in the first survey, and the results were eye-opening. From the data returned by his ground troops, Mayfield learned that there were 432 singing males. Assuming that each male had a mate, that would mean that the total population of the Kirtland's warbler was likely fewer than 1,000 birds. Furthermore, Mayfield deduced that much of the conventional wisdom about plots thought to be suitable for nesting habitat was wrong. By comparing the location of the nests with the size of the plot, Mayfield concluded that the warbler prefers to nest in large, loose groups, with each male requiring his own territory. It was now clear to Mayfield that many of the plots that had been planted specifically for the Kirtland's simply weren't big enough.

Although many people have remarked previously that the bird has not utilized nearly all the seemingly suitable habitat, we have not appreciated before how large a tract of land with suitable cover is the minimum utilized by nesting birds. From the data supplied thus far, there is only one record of Kirtland's Warblers on tracts of less than 60 acres and there are very few on tracts smaller than 80 acres (that is, if rectangular, one-half mile by one-quarter mile).

I examined one strip of jack pines one and one-half miles long and 150 yards wide, with an abrupt transition to totally unsuitable area at the edges. It contained no Kirtland's although there were many colonies in seemingly identical cover in the same township. My only explanation is that this strip was too narrow.

The large "minimum area" is all the more surprising in view of the fact that the territory of a singing male is only one to four acres, and the male and female rarely leave their own territory during nesting season.

In the sections that contained birds, there was an average of 33 acres of apparently suitable land for each singing male (based on data supplied for 319 males on a total estimated acreage of 10,710). In Oscoda County the colonies I examined averaged one male for each 29 acres of plantings.[20]

From the census, Mayfield also reached two other important conclusions.

Even though the warblers want to nest among thick jack pines, they want thickets and openings near their nests.
Even though the warblers prefer jack pines, they will accept red pines. The problem with red pines is that they rarely grow

close enough together for their lower branches to overlap and provide the kind of shelter the warbler seeks.

The results of the 1951 census motivated foresters and wildlife biologists to commit more land to the warbler. They would soon find that it still wouldn't be enough.

If the mood wasn't one of panic in an Ann Arbor meeting room on a late October afternoon in 1971, it was awfully close. Representatives of the Michigan Department of Natural Resources (DNR), the U.S. Forest Service, the U.S. Fish and Wildlife Service, the University of Michigan, and various Audubon societies gathered to review the results of the third Kirtland's warbler census, which had been conducted five months earlier. The numbers were bleak.

The second census, conducted in 1961, had actually showed the Kirtland's population growing slightly, to 502 singing males. The 1971 census, however, found only 201 singing males, meaning that in the ten years since the 1961 census, the Kirtland's warbler population had dropped by 60 percent. The reasons for the drop were obvious to everybody in the room. First, vast areas of jack pine forest had been allowed to mature beyond suitable Kirtland's warbler nesting habitat. With wildfires being controlled to prevent damage to private property and potential wood products, the tracts of jack pine that did occasionally burn usually weren't large enough to attract a warbler colony. The next problem was the cowbird. Dr. Nicholas Cuthbert of Central Michigan University and Bruce Radabaugh of the Pontiac Audubon Society documented that in the 1960s, 83 percent of the Kirtland's warblers' nests were being parasitized by cowbirds annually.[21] That rate of parasitism meant the average Kirtland's warbler's nest fledged .81 birds per pair of adults.[22] At that rate, the Kirtland's warbler was headed rapidly for extinction. Based on the high rate of parasitism, Cuthbert speculated that cowbirds might be species specific in that female cowbirds reared by Kirtland's warblers would intentionally seek out Kirtland's warbler nests to parasitize when it came time to lay their own eggs.

Recognizing the danger posed by the cowbird, Cuthbert had spent the previous decade experimenting with various methods to trap, shoot, and poison them. He concluded that trapping was the best method for removing cowbirds from the habitat after studies in two Kirtland's nesting areas had cut cowbird nest parasitism to 21 percent. From 1966 to 1971, Walkinshaw also studied the effect of the traps on three Kirtland's nesting areas and discovered that not only did the traps cut the rate of cowbird parasitism, but the average number of Kirtland's eggs per nest increased from 2.34 to 4.22. Even better, the average number of young Kirtland's fledged increased from .81 in nontrapping areas to 2.84 in areas where cowbirds were trapped.[23]

Everyone in the room believed that it was time to take action against the cowbird, but they needed to develop a complete strategy. Before the participants left that afternoon, the group formed themselves into the Kirtland's Warbler Advisory Committee and various members were charged with a task: create a comprehensive plan to revive the warbler population and have it ready in just ten days.

The group met again in Ann Arbor in early November, and in just a little more than a week the mood had switched from panic to resolve. Before the meeting ended, the committee had established a five-point recovery plan. First, the Fish and Wildlife Service would start a cowbird control program in all active Kirtland's warbler nesting areas. Two locals would be hired to monitor the traps on a daily basis at a rate of three dollars an hour. Second, both the state of Michigan and the Forest Service would accelerate their efforts to acquire and set aside more land to expand the amount of protected jack pine forest. Third, both the state and the Forest Service would establish a rotation program to ensure the warbler would always have adequate nesting habitat. Fourth, the committee would establish a subcommittee to oversee research. Fifth, all research on the Kirtland's would be published and shared.

Action was swift. In the spring of 1972, the Fish and Wildlife Service set up thirteen cowbird traps, which would function from May 1 through July 15. Traps were built out of wood and chicken wire with an entrance on top designed so that a cowbird could drop in to eat food placed inside. The traps then were stocked with lures—live cowbirds that had been captured in late April in Ohio and shipped north. Because cowbirds are gregarious and tend to want to be with other cowbirds, they will voluntarily enter a cage through a small trap door when they see that there's also food and water inside. Anticipating that other species would accidentally enter the cage—hawks and falcons looking for easy meals—volunteers were recruited to monitor the traps daily.

Deciding where to set up the traps was easy, since the 1971 census showed that nearly the entire population of the Kirtland's warbler had collapsed to the center of its historic nesting range.

The trapping program had an immediate and dramatic impact. Since 1972, more than four thousand cowbirds a year on average have been removed from the Kirtland's nesting habitat,[24] and, as a result, the warbler's nesting success rate has increased dramatically. Prior to cowbird trapping, Walkinshaw figured that the cowbird parasitism rate was just under 70 percent and the Kirtland's warbler nesting success rate was 0.81 birds per nest. After cowbird trapping began, the parasitism rate dropped to less than 10 percent and the nesting success rate jumped to more than three birds per nest.[25]

To monitor the effectiveness of the cowbird trapping, the Fish and Wildlife Service hired Walkinshaw to monitor the Kirtland's warbler nests for parasitism. Unable to find many cowbird eggs in Kirtland's warbler nests, Walkinshaw quit after just a couple years because, he said, he didn't want to disturb nests when he knew he wasn't going to find anything. Wanting to continue the nest monitoring, the Fish and Wildlife Service hired Nicholas Cuthbert, who quit the job after one field season for the same reason—so few cowbird eggs were found that the human disturbance to the nesting Kirtland's warblers just wasn't worth it.

Mike Petrucha, now a wildlife assistant with the Michigan Department of Natural Resources, spent four years working on the cowbird-trapping program in the early 1990s. Petrucha's various duties included coordinating seasonal employees and volunteers to remove excess cowbirds from the traps and showing the public how the cowbird-trapping program works. When asked by bird-watchers and tourists what happened to cowbirds caught in the traps, Petrucha would tell them that he sends them to a "different" habitat. When the public

Mike Petrucha explains the trapping of brown-headed cowbirds to a group visiting the Kirtland's Warbler Wildlife Festival.

wasn't around, Petrucha disposed of the cowbirds by snapping their necks and burying their bodies. In a macabre way it was a position that brought Petrucha a high level of job satisfaction.

"I felt I was really helping an endangered species produce young," Petrucha said.

Weinrich, who also has spent his share of time in cowbird traps, says there are three different ways to humanely kill a cowbird: cervical dislocation, thoracic compression, and cranial concussion. Weinrich now also realizes that there's karma involved in killing a cowbird, at least when you use the cranial concussion method. To kill a cowbird using this method, you hold the bird in your hand, facing toward you. You then fracture the bird's skull by hitting its head against the wooden frame of the trap in a motion that is similar to swinging a hammer. Weinrich no longer uses this technique because the action of striking the bird's head on the wood caused the head to swing forward and drive its beak deep into his hand.

There was one other reward for taking cowbirds out of the habitat:

At the end of each season in which he worked on the traps, Petrucha organized a picnic to thank his workers. As a surprise, he would serve them beer, bratwurst, and cowbird. Each cowbird yielded two chicken-nugget-sized breasts, which Petrucha floured, sprinkled with a little salt and pepper, and fried in olive oil. Of twenty-five employees and volunteers, only two declined to try it. One was a vegetarian and the other later expressed regret.

The formation of the Kirtland's Warbler Advisory Committee was significant for two reasons. First, the quick action and resolve of its members likely saved the Kirtland's warbler from extinction. Second, committee members created the vision and a culture of cooperation that was then adopted by the Kirtland's Warbler Recovery Team, which was formed as a result of the passage of the Endangered Species Act in 1973. The vision and cooperative spirit established by the advisory committee were behind the three key recommendations in the comprehensive recovery plan in 1976: interagency responsibility for cowbird control, habitat management, and public education. With so much on the line, turf fights would not be tolerated.

With cowbirds now being controlled, a comprehensive conservation plan in place, and so much progress being made on so many other fronts, why wasn't the Kirtland's warbler population growing? Cowbird trapping and population modeling helped biologists understand that when it came to reproduction, the Kirtland's warbler was not only very productive, but it had a high first-year survival rate. If more birds were being hatched, that meant that more birds were surviving. But if more birds were surviving, why were the census numbers still flat?

Cowbird trapping prevented the Kirtland's warbler's quick extinction. But what biologists and foresters still did not understand was that the population was still stuck in a bottleneck because of a lack of adequate nesting habitat. As wildlife biologists and foresters worked to create habitat on a small scale, the Kirtland's warbler's real nesting needs would become apparent only after a tragic accident.

FOUR : Guinea Pigs

With still so little known about the Kirtland's warbler in the early 1950s, Josselyn Van Tyne, Harold Mayfield, and their research colleagues struggled to find a solution that would guarantee the bird's survival. So who could blame them if they sometimes made unusual decisions, took risks, or made things up as they went along?

One of the more unusual steps Van Tyne and Mayfield took was to try to hand raise Kirtland's warblers in captivity. At least once, both Van Tyne and Mayfield took nestlings back to their homes in Ann Arbor and Toledo. Unfortunately, neither had success raising these birds, and understandably they did not document their efforts.

Knowing he had not had success raising a Kirtland's warbler, Van Tyne turned to Andrew Berger, one of his research colleagues, because Berger was already studying several species of wild birds in captivity in his home in Ann Arbor.

Although Berger and Van Tyne spent many hours together in the field, the two shared few personality traits. While Van Tyne was the alpha male—focused, organized, rigid, uncompromising, and driven—Berger was eclectic and easygoing. Unlike Van Tyne, who was focused only on birds, Berger had an incredibly wide range of knowledge. Berger taught anatomy at the University of Michigan School of Medicine, but his first love was birds, so much so that, in 1964, his boss told him he would have to make a choice: give up birds in order to focus on his teaching or leave. The decision was easy; Berger immediately took a position in the Department of Zoology at the University of Hawai'i.

Although Van Tyne and Berger share credit for authoring the classic book *Fundamentals of Ornithology,* Berger's name was added to the volume only out of necessity. In 1956, Berger was with Van Tyne on a research plot near Mack Lake, Michigan, when Van Tyne was stricken with chest pains. On the spot, Van Tyne made Berger promise to complete the manuscript if he should die before it was completed.[1] Less than a year later, when Van Tyne did indeed die, Berger stayed true to his word. The day after Van Tyne's death on January 30, 1957, Berger showed up on Van Tyne's porch and asked for the manuscript from Van Tyne's wife, Helen. At that moment, Helen Van Tyne developed a hatred for Berger that lasted the rest of her life.

Berger's first attempt to raise a Kirtland's warbler was a single seven-day-old bird that he took from a nest of four in July 1956. Berger transferred the warbler to a screened breezeway that connected his Ann Arbor rental house to its garage. When Berger was displaced from the rental house the next month, he kept the warbler in a cage in his medical school office and often let it out to hop around his desk. In early 1957, Berger and his family moved into a new home with an indoor aviary. Before the summer was over Berger had built three outdoor cages and attached them to the indoor aviary via a window. In the outdoor cages, Berger planted variety of native vegetation, including raspberry, elderberry, gray dogwood, ninebark, honeysuckle, and wild grape. Those plants not only provided direct food for the birds, but their flowers and overly mature fruit attracted insects for the birds to eat.

With the summer off from teaching, Berger could devote more than fifteen hours a day to observing the young warbler and recording its development. He wrote that taking the birds from the nest just about the time the feathers are starting to develop is the optimum age because the birds have yet to develop a fear reaction. Prior to the development of the fear reaction, "the nestlings will raise their heads high and gape widely when an observer 'squeaks' or taps the rim of the nest with his finger or a stick." But once the fear reaction develops, the nestlings will crouch down and hide when the nest is approached.[2]

The young warbler received a diet of hard-boiled egg whites, red raspberries, bananas, mealworms, and a wide variety of insects, plus small quantities of bread soaked in milk. When the bird was approximately two weeks old, Berger added mashed hard-boiled egg, grated raw carrot, and either water or condensed milk.[3]

Berger collected additional birds in 1958 and 1963 and made even more detailed observations of their development. The birds quickly learned that a whistle meant it was feeding time, and on hearing the sound they would promptly perch on Berger's head, shoulder, or hand. He observed that by the time these birds were two weeks old they were already attempting to pick up food, including insects they found in their aviary. (One bird in particular went an entire day with the mandibles of a dead black ant securely clamped to the tip of its tongue. Berger finally removed the mandibles after several attempts.) By the time the birds were twenty-one days old, they were able to discriminate between insects they liked to eat and ones they did not.

Berger made detailed descriptions of how the young voided fecal sacs while in the nest. He noted sleeping behavior and how many days it took the young birds to develop the neuromuscular strength to sleep with their heads turned around to rest on the scapular feathers. He noted the development of the mechanism that enables a bird to hold its grasp on a perch. He also recorded how a Kirtland's warbler ate a beetle, first picking off the legs, then pecking off the head and eating parts of it, then attacking the rest of the insect, shaking it and pounding it against the floor until the wing covers came off. The bird would then run the thorax and abdomen back and forth between its mandibles "for some time before swallowing the limp remains."

Alas, Berger was able to keep each of the warblers alive for only a few months, and he and other researchers eventually concluded that Kirtland's warblers could not be raised in captivity. Ultimately the experiment has to be considered a failure, and Berger's keen observations will have a minimal impact on science. But it was worth a try.

FIVE : "Now We've Got a Problem"

May 5, 1980, dawned a glorious spring morning. The sky was a crisp azure, the wind was calm, and the daytime high temperature was headed for the low eighties. After a fairly bleak April that saw lingering snowfall and overnight temperatures regularly below freezing, five straight days of sunshine and growing warmth to open May had the earth and its residents finally stirring.

After a long winter of making plans, the employees of U.S. Forest Service office in Mio, Michigan, decided it was time to get to work. Topping their to-do list was the cleanup of a two-hundred-acre plot of jack pine in the Huron National Forest about five miles south of town. The area had been set aside as a future nesting site for the Kirtland's warbler and had been clear-cut the previous fall. But before the area could be replanted with young jack pine, it needed to be cleared of slash—the branches, needles, and stumps that had been left behind. The best way to clear the area, in Forest Service lingo, would be to conduct a "controlled burn." A controlled burn was no big deal, as both the Forest Service and the Michigan Department of Natural Resources had been intentionally setting fire to small areas for the Kirtland's warbler since the early 1960s. Both the Forest Service and the DNR had developed rules to govern these controlled burns. Each one was carefully planned in advance, and personnel and equipment were always on location and ready to deal with any emergency.

Both agencies were under pressure to conduct burns this spring. The 1979 Kirtland's warbler census had found only slightly more than two hundred singing males, and the population had been nearly flat for the previous decade. The longer the population stayed at this level, the higher the risk of extinction grew. And with wildlife biologists now possessing a better understanding of how much space a colony of Kirtland's warblers needs, there was pressure to make more nesting habitat available. The best way to grow the warbler's population, the biologists reasoned, would be to provide more nesting habitat.

On this morning, conditions were excellent for a fire; low humidity and no rain during the previous four days had combined to make the slash—and the rest of the forest—tinder dry. Both the Forest Service and the DNR checked the weather forecast that morning: the afternoon would bring a cold front down from the northwest, with strong winds, clouds, cooler temperatures, and occasional rain showers. In light of the forecast for strong winds, the DNR canceled its burn. But the Forest Service gave the go-ahead because managers expected the burn to be completed before the strong winds would arrive.[1]

Aware of the risk any fire brings, the Forest Service had placed firefighting equipment—a tractor plow and a thousand-gallon water tanker truck—at the scene and had plowed a firebreak around the perimeter. Forest Service workers also made calls to residents in the area to notify them of the prescribed burn. There was no reason to panic if they saw smoke, they were told.

Unfortunately, four critical elements were missing from the Forest Service's plan. First, there was no way for Forest Service workers to communicate reliably among themselves or with the headquarters. The burn site was in a location that was a known dead spot for radio transmissions. Second, one piece of equipment—a thousand-gallon water tanker truck that would be critical to containing and controlling the fire—regularly stalled and was notoriously unreliable. Third, the district's fire officer, Clifford Reedy, whose job it was to manage all forest fires in the area, was elsewhere. Fourth, three members of the burn crew were away attending law enforcement school, which meant the remaining crew would be shorthanded. Since the crew was shorthanded, Forest Service biological technician James Swiderski volunteered to operate the tractor plow, even though he was a biologist and not certified to use the machine.

At 10:26 a.m., before climbing aboard the tractor plow, Swiderski used a drip torch to light a fire on the western side of the plot.

At the same time, about five miles away, just outside the tiny community of Mack Lake, Frank Cowger, a retired newspaper photographer from the *Detroit News,* headed out to work in his yard. Cowger was eager to get his chores done because he was aware of the weather forecast. Once outside, he glanced to the west and was relieved to see that the smoke from the controlled burn was going straight up. A few minutes later, he noticed the wind picking up and looked up to see that the smoke from the burn was thick, black, and rapidly blowing off to the east.

His first thought was, "Now we've got a problem."

Fire—whether caused by lightning or humans—has been part of the northern Michigan jack pine forest for at least ten thousand years. Although there is no way to be certain, it's believed that Native Americans set fire to the forest—either deliberately or accidentally—for hundreds of years before the arrival of Europeans. The newly created openings in the forest attracted animals that would then be hunted for food. To the Native Americans, fire was a tool of survival. Today humans see a stand of charred tree trunks and tend to think of it as an eyesore or a tragedy. But these natural disturbances are a fundamental part of the ecology of the Kirtland's warbler's ecosystem. The warbler and the other plants and animals in this area have not just adapted to fire; they have come to depend on it. But no species in this ecosystem requires fire more than the jack pine. A jack pine's seeds are sealed inside its cones by a resinous bond that will break down under intense heat. The cones themselves usually remain undamaged by the heat because fire moves through the tree so quickly. After the fire, the wind can disperse the winged seeds onto the ash-rich ground as far as 130 feet from the tree. And because fire is an irregular occurrence, jack pine seeds remain viable in the cone for decades.[2] Young jack pines grow slowly for the first four years, putting much of their energy into expanding their root structure. They begin to grow cones when they are between three and five years old, as the trees prepare for the next round of fire. In areas where fire traditionally has occurred frequently, the fast-growing jack pine quickly became the dominant tree species.

A 1983 study found that large fires in excess of ten thousand acres occurred on average every twenty-eight years prior to European settlement,[3] and the U.S. Forest Service considers jack pine to be one of the most volatile and dangerous fuel types in the United States.[4] The jack pine is built to burn. Once a fire starts on the ground, grasses and other vegetation carry flames upward to the tree's crown. Fire is intensified by the tree's flammable sap, which concentrates over the winter into a liquid that is similar to turpentine. Late April and early May are the most dangerous times for fire in these woods; the snow has melted, but many of the plants are still dormant and tinder dry. After the trees and ground vegetation come out of dormancy and begin to take in water, the fire danger decreases significantly. But once a fire becomes established in a stand of jack pines it is difficult to control. Hot updrafts carry tiny pieces of burning wood and cones into the air to start new fires downwind. Firefighters avoid getting caught in front of a crown fire at all cost. Instead, they try to control the fire's flanks until the crown fire drops back down to the ground.

Jack pines can burn so completely that sometimes all that is left after a fire is a stand of charred trunks and limbs. With the branches and needles largely gone and the ground covered in nutrient-rich ash, the stage is set for a rapid regeneration. With no tall trees to block the light, the sunlight shines directly on the ground, and jack pine seedlings and a lush layer of resprouting ground plants spring up in just a few weeks.

The jack pine is one of the most common trees in northern North America. A jack pine belt stretches across Canada from the Rockies to the Atlantic Ocean, and extends south into northern Michigan and as far north as Hudson Bay. The jack pine is able to live on the thin, acidic soil of the Canadian Shield, on rocky outcrops on mountainsides, and in wet riverbeds. So with all these jack pines across North America, why does the Kirtland's nest where it does? The answer is in the ground.

Take a map of all the soil types in Wisconsin, Michigan, and Ontario

Map 1. The Kirtland warbler's breeding range in Michigan's northern Lower Peninsula

and lay a map of all the known Kirtland's warblers' nests over the top. More than 90 percent of the nests will be in one small area of northern Michigan some seventy-five miles from north to south and one hundred miles from east to west. That's because much of the soil there is composed of Grayling sand. The low branches of the jack pine provide cover for a Kirtland's warbler nest, but the combination of jack pines and this sandy, well-draining soil, which rarely floods and provides dense groundcover, may be the ultimate draw for a bird that nests on the ground.

These sandy soils were deposited ten to fourteen thousand years ago as a great glacier advanced and receded over much of North America. As the mile-thick glacier advanced and receded with changes in the weather, it pushed up and deposited hills called moraines. And each time the glacier receded, melting water carried sand and gravel away from the moraines to be deposited in low areas between them. Not much is able to grow in this nutrient-poor sand; few deciduous trees can make it—northern pin oak, black cherry, and the rare Allegheny plum are exceptions. And in Oscoda and Crawford counties in northeastern Michigan, where the warbler nests in abundance, the climate further inhibits the growth of deciduous trees. Much of the Kirtland's warbler nesting ground is on a high plateau that keeps the climate from being moderated by Lake Michigan to the west. This causes average daytime temperatures to be one degree Fahrenheit hotter during the day and two degrees cooler at night compared to nearby areas off the plateau, with extremes often occurring on windless days and nights.[5] The colder overnight temperature, in particular, has a profound impact. In the area that may be the single most important nesting habitat for the Kirtland's warbler, overnight lows can fall below freezing even in the hottest months of summer. Despite the cold microclimate, the jack pine thrives here, along with Pennsylvania sedge, various grasses, three species of blueberries, sweet fern, ram's head lady slipper, wood lily, and threatened plants like the prairie dandelion and Hill's thistle. This ankle-high ground layer provides the cover for the Kirtland's nest. Few of these plants can grow in the shade of adult jack pines, and they will die when the trees become so tall and thick that they monopolize the sun. They will also come back as strong as ever immediately after the next disturbance by resprouting from their root systems.

Compared to wetlands or deciduous edge habitat, animal life in the jack pine ecosystem is relative sparse. Coyotes like it because it supports a healthy mouse and vole population. The Allegheny ant builds huge colonies, digging tunnels as deep as twelve feet below the surface. Michigan's only endemic grasshopper, the barrens locust, is also found here. Three varieties of blueberries draw black bears during the summer. Brewer's blackbirds, upland sandpipers, common nighthawks, and snowshoe hares all use the youngest jack pines. New groups of animals will move in as the trees age. Eastern bluebirds; indigo buntings; chipping, clay-colored, Lincoln's, savannah, and vesper sparrows; yellow-rumped and Nashville warblers; hermit thrushes; spruce grouse; and brown thrashers will use jack pines when the trees are less than fifteen years old. A jack pine is short-lived compared with red and white pines. The tree is fully mature at sixty years and can stand as tall as sixty-five feet. At this age, the jack pine forest is used by the northern goshawk, but now the jack pines are at the end of their life span.

After fire sweeps through a mature jack pine stand, the charred trees support another rare species, the black-backed woodpecker, which feeds on bark beetle larvae in the dead trees for the first few years after a fire.

Although there are no numbers, it is likely that raging fires in the late nineteenth century led to a bubble in the Kirtland's population. Demand for wood grew rapidly after the Civil War as the American population expanded into the Midwest and Great Plains. With demand for wood products outstripping the supply of trees in New York and New England, a fast-growing nation turned to Michigan for wood with which to build houses, ships, carriages, and railroads. From the time commercial logging started in Michigan in the 1830s through the 1870s, the bulk of the cutting was limited to the winter; it was far easier to move logs from the forest to the sawmill on sleds when the ground was frozen.

Two technological advances at this time allowed the lumbermen to accelerate the logging: the crosscut saw replaced the ax as the tree-felling tool of choice, and the expansion of narrow-gauge railroads into the wilderness allowed lumbermen to increase both the speed and amount of wood taken to the sawmill. Lumbering in Michigan peaked in the 1890s, and by 1910 the Lower Peninsula's primeval red and white pine forests were gone. Because the lumbermen viewed the wood as inexhaustible, they often took only the choice parts of the tree, leaving behind vast areas of stumps, trunks, limbs, branches, needles, and other debris.[6] They also left behind jack pine trees, which were considered to be worthless because of the poor quality of the wood.

With forests disappearing, farmers looked to take advantage of the newly cleared land. Before they could farm, however, they needed to clear the land of all the remaining wood. And the quickest way to do that was to burn it. At any one time there were hundreds if not thousands of small fires burning across northern Michigan, a thick smoke often covered vast sections of the state. Fire now became an even bigger part of the northern Michigan landscape, and it took a terrible human toll.

On October 8, 1871, the same day as the great Chicago fire, a wildfire started on the eastern shore of Lake Michigan. It destroyed the towns of Holland and Manistee and burned across the state, stopping only at the shore of Lake Huron. The fire burned more than one million acres, including many stands of virgin white pine.

On October 15, 1908, an open train car carrying people attempting to flee a wildfire in Presque Isle County derailed in the middle of intense flames. Sixteen people were killed and dozens more severely burned.

In 1910, Rose City burned to the ground in less than an hour—save for two buildings made of concrete.

On July 11, 1911, a massive wall of fire, driven by winds gusting at fifty miles per hour, roared into the neighboring lumber mill towns of Oscoda and AuSable on the Au Sable River's mouth at Lake Huron. Nearly everything was wiped out by the fast-moving flames. The people and animals that could escape fled first to the shoreline and then plunged neck deep into the rough lake water. Flames from the dying town were so intense that survivors were forced to splash water on their heads to keep their hair and foreheads from burning. Trapped by flames in AuSable, a few people and animals fled to the docks where they were lucky to escape on a lumber boat that had pulled in to the dock just as the fire began to sweep through town. Although it took only a few minutes to load the boat, both the aft and fore cabins of the ship were on fire by the time it left the dock.

The fire's ghastly toll at AuSable and Oscoda forced the state government to act: In 1912, Michigan's Public Domain Commission, the forerunner to today's Department of Natural Resources, purchased eighteen long-handled shovels to equip firefighters, and modern fire suppression techniques were introduced to Michigan. With the land opened up, agriculture moved in—and almost immediately failed due to the sandy soil and microclimate. With the land reverting to the state and federal governments, large areas that had been jack pine land were replaced with more economically desirable white and red pines. And with humans aggressively fighting forest fires, more jack pine trees were able to reach maturity. With the forest aging and the impact of the brown-headed cowbird, the Kirtland's warbler population headed for a crash.

Following the 1951 census, small-scale efforts were made to

increase warbler habitat on land owned by the Michigan Department of Natural Resources and the U.S. Forest Service. In 1956, the Michigan Conservation Commission, at the urging of Harold Mayfield and others, voted unanimously to have the state's forestry department establish a Kirtland's warbler preserve, so as to, in Mayfield's words, "not leave the future of the Kirtland's warbler to chance."[7] In 1957, the Conservation Department started managing small tracts specifically for the Kirtland's warbler, but in many ways, people making decisions on the future of the species made up things up as they went along.

"No regrets," says Bill Irvine, a retired U.S. Forest Service wildlife biologist and a founding member of the Kirtland's Warbler Advisory Committee. "It's just a fact of life that we didn't have good definitive studies to develop a habitat plan." Irvine says he now understands that early attempts at managing Kirtland's warbler habitat weren't successful for several reasons.

> Wildlife biologists believed that the warbler would nest only under jack pine trees and on Grayling sand soil. Foresters limited their warbler management efforts to areas that turned out to be artificially small.
>
> The jack pine was not rotated quickly enough to provide a constant new supply of prime nesting habitat.
>
> The plots that did offer prime nesting habitat were often too small to attract a colony. Despite setting aside more than eleven thousand acres for the warbler in the early 1960s, the Forest Service burned only a one-square-mile block at a time. That meant that only a small percentage of Kirtland's warbler management land was actually prime nesting habitat in any one year.
>
> Not understanding the importance of deciduous trees to the Kirtland's warbler, plots were cleared of all woody plants and replanted exclusively with jack pines. The result was an unappealing jack pine monoculture.
>
> Not understanding the warbler's need for forest edges and open space, foresters planted new jack pines too tightly and failed to leave openings.

In the earliest days of Kirtland's warbler research, biologists didn't even understand or appreciate fire's role in creating nesting habitat. Twenty-two years after discovering the first Kirtland's warbler nest, Norman Wood returned to northern Michigan to follow up on his earlier work. However, when he arrived in an area in Clare County that had been a Kirtland's warbler colony in previous years, he found the area had been destroyed by fire. After driving across northern lower Michigan for a couple of days and finding that two more nesting areas had been destroyed by fire, Wood concluded that fire was a threat: "Fire is without doubt the greatest menace to the Kirtland Warbler colonies, since it destroys the habitat as well as the nests of the birds. . . . The Cowbird probably destroys large numbers of eggs—but is not so serious a problem for the warbler as fire."[8]

By the time Irvine and his colleagues began to manage for the Kirtland's warbler, however, biologists had a much better understanding of the traditional role that fire played in the ecosystem, and they decided that they would harness it as one of their tools. In 1964, Les Line, then the outdoors editor of the *Midland Daily News,* explained in *Audubon* that when it came to preventing the extinction of the Kirtland's warbler, fire was the natural choice.

> The embers were still smoldering when the first prescribed burn for the benefit of a songbird was declared a success by Louis A. Pommerening, Huron-Manistee forest supervisor. By late summer, he predicted tiny jack-pine seedlings would be sprouting where blackened, freshly popped cones were scattered. Kirtland's warblers, he added, could be expected to be nesting there again within five to ten years. By then, other woods would be ready for firing nearby.[9]

The fire was called the "Pop Cone Project," and it was also used as a training session for new wildfire fighting equipment that distributed sand to bury a ground fire and a "jelled" water chemical that was dropped on the fire from airplanes and sprayed from other equipment on the ground.

Firefighters desperately needed to upgrade their training and equipment because more people from downstate were building cottages and cabins in the area and the year-round population was slowly growing as downstate retirees were choosing quiet solitude over the congestion of the city. That meant more houses were being built and communities were expanding in the middle of the tinderbox that is a mature jack pine forest.

The May 5 prescribed burn went according to plan for the first hour and a half. The ground fire burned vigorously, with flame heights reaching fifteen feet, fed by southwesterly winds between five and twelve miles per hour.[10] Spot fires, ignited by flying embers, were anticipated outside the area of the prescribed burn, and Forest Service workers quickly controlled them with tractor plows when they were discovered. But shortly after noon, the approaching cold front began to exert its influence and winds began to build. Fire workers noticed a fast-moving spot fire in a mature jack pine stand adjacent to the prescribed burn area and moved quickly to plow a firebreak between the fire and M-33, the main road into Mio from the south. While fighting this fire, the water tanker got stuck on a hillside tree stump inside the burn area. With fire bearing down on the tanker, its operators radioed Swiderski to come and pull them off with the tractor plow. A few minutes later the notoriously unreliable tanker stalled. With its operator unable to restart the vehicle, Swiderski was again diverted from fighting the fire to pull the tanker away from approaching flames to a safe spot on a nearby road. While Swiderski was rescuing his colleagues and their vehicle, another spot fire was discovered around 12:15, this time east of M-33. Swiderski quickly attacked this fire, and the crew had it contained when yet another spot fire broke out. Now it was too late. This fire quickly spread as if it were climbing a ladder, going from young jack pine to older and larger trees and finally into the crowns of mature jack pine. It was now out of control.

At 12:30 the Forest Service's manager on the burn radioed the district station for additional manpower, including an aerial spotter. By 12:35, the leading edge of the windblown fire was already a half mile east of M-33, and flaming embers were starting even more fires downwind of the fire's main line. With the wind now variable from the south and west, the fire's north flank often acted as if it were the head of the fire. In the Forest Service's official report, fire crews later recalled that the fire was very sensitive to changes in wind direction, and with each shift the flanks of the fire that had been under control would suddenly explode. Flames on the ground were now as high as forty feet, and flame tops in the crown fire reached as high as two hundred feet.[11]

On the north edge of the fire, Swiderski began to plow a west-to-east firebreak through heavy, roiling black smoke.[12] As he desperately worked, a crew driving an armored tanker passed him, moving ahead to spray the ground with water.[13] It was the last time anyone would see Swiderski alive.

No one actually saw Swiderski's tractor become engulfed. In an attempt to escape flames approaching from the south, Swiderski turned his tractor north, which was right in the path of a fast-moving crown fire approaching from the west. In a desperate attempt to escape, Swiderski abandoned his tractor and tried to run for it.

By 1:00 p.m., word was out that the fire was out of control and spreading quickly. The Forest Service mobilized additional fire crews and equipment from Minnesota, Wisconsin, and Missouri, and members of the Michigan National Guard from nearby Camp Grayling joined the fight. Jim Davisson, editor of the *Oscoda County News*, drove rapidly from one remote home to another warning residents to get out.[14]

Driven by winds now gusting to twenty-five miles per hour, the fire rapidly approached the community of Mack Lake. Seeing a wall of fire stretching from the ground to more than twenty feet above the treetops, residents took what they could gather and fled. In the town of Oscoda, Michigan, thirty-five miles downwind of the fire, smoke filled the air and ashes as large as half an inch fell from the sky.

Around 3:00 p.m., the spotter plane sighted Swiderski's burned tractor plow. Meanwhile, on the ground in the wake of the fire, Randy Marzolo, a Forest Service employee, searched through the burned trunks and embers for Swiderski. Eventually, he found Swiderski's burned body about three hundred feet from the plow.

Around 4:30 p.m., as the fire was bearing down on the small community of South Branch, fire crews finally caught a break. The passage of the cold front brought higher humidity, which helped diminish the fire's intensity and slow its progress. At about the same time, the north flank of the fire ran out of jack pine as it moved into hardwood trees growing on a moraine. Without highly combustible jack pine needles and sap to feed the flames, the swift-moving crown fire died, allowing firefighters to deal with a much less intense ground fire. By midnight, the fire had spread only an additional half mile to the east and south. Crews worked throughout the night to plow a thirty-five-mile firebreak. Within a few hours, the fire would be out.

With the fire under control, the Forest Service started to focus on damage control. The phones at the its office in Mio were ringing steadily as news organizations from Bay City, Saginaw, and Detroit began to call with questions. They all wanted to know the answer to the same question: did the government really start this fire?

The phone rang in Dick Klade's home in Milwaukee on the evening of May 5. Klade was the Forest Service's public information officer for the eastern United States, and his supervisor was calling to tell him that he needed to be on a plane bound for northern Michigan first thing in the next morning. "Here we go again," he thought. Klade had built a career on heading out the door on a moment's notice. He previously had been the Forest Service's point man for forest fire information in Boise, Idaho, where fires were much more common and widespread than in the Great Lakes region. A fire information assignment in the West meant that Klade could be on the road for more than ten days at a time.

Early on May 6, Klade hopped a Forest Service plane to Cadillac, Michigan, where he was met by Wayne Mann, supervisor of the Huron-Manistee National Forests. On the rushed drive back to Mio, Mann briefed Klade on the situation and gave him specific instructions on what to say—and what not to say. When the two reached Mio, they discovered the headquarters crowded with regular employees, professional fire management people, and about a dozen residents of Mack Lake whose homes had been damaged or destroyed by the fire. Klade's first job was to reassure the homeowners that the very same government that had just burned them out of their homes would now treat them fairly. Lucky for him, the Forest Service staff had already thrown water on another flammable situation; the staff had gathered the residents at the headquarters and got them started on the process of filing claims for compensation. Klade credits this quick action with mitigating the property owners' anger. Ironically, Klade recalls that the loudest complaints he received came from a group of local volunteer firefighters who were angry that the Forest Service had refused to let them help. Klade says the Forest Service decided to keep the volunteers out for safety reasons and maintains to this day that administrators did the right thing. "The early part of the Mack Lake fire featured very swift and erratic movement of the flames," Klade said. "It was no place for people to be who were not specifically trained to handle wildfire situations."

The fire took a tremendous toll on the landscape, but it also took an emotional toll on the residents of both Mio and Mack Lake. Even though the fire was out, a cloud of acrid smoke, symbolic of the mood, hung over Mio for a week. Mio residents were stunned and saddened by Swiderski's death, but they were also mad as hell at the government.

Ed Miller, a young reporter for the Associated Press (AP), was working the news desk at the Detroit bureau when a phone call about the Mack Lake fire came in from a radio reporter in Saginaw. Miller already knew about other fires burning in Michigan but immediately realized that the Mack Lake fire was far more newsworthy and rushed to gather facts and post a story on the AP wire. The next day, that story was published in newspapers around the world, including the *New York Times* and the *Australian*. Miller recalls that shortly after the story ran in Australia, he received phone calls and letters from people in that country wanting to know more about the Kirtland's warbler. Realizing that this story was bigger than its parts, Miller went to his boss to propose that he go to the Mio area to write a series of follow-up stories.

"I had to beg the boss to go," says Miller, who is now a public relations executive with American Honda.

By the time Miller got to Mio, nearly a month after the fire, he found people there still angry and upset. Miller says that he would stop for gasoline or a meal and tell people why he was in the Mio area, and they would just explode with anger.

Mention the fire to Ed Faussett today and he only goes into a slow burn. Nearly thirty years after the event, time has tempered his emotions somewhat, but he isn't hesitant to share his feelings about the fire, the Forest Service, or the Kirtland's warbler. He and his wife, Mary Jane, keep a large envelope full of now brown and fragile press clippings about the fire. Originally from Canton Township, Michigan, a far western Detroit suburb, the Faussetts live in one of Mack Lake's nicest homes; it's the only one in town with an adjoining tennis court. In 1989, Ed and Mary Jane moved to Mack Lake to become full-time summer residents after Ed retired from Northwest Airlines. Ed had been coming to the area for several years to hunt and fish with his family before he and Mary Jane bought their first Mack Lake home in 1968. It was a small house just a little way down the hill from where they live today. Like so many other downstate residents, they cherished the quiet and seclusion of their northern Michigan home on long weekends and during summer vacations.

After hearing about the fire from the Detroit news media, Ed and Mary Jane made plans to go to Mack Lake as soon as possible to check on their house. They arrived two days later to find it untouched by the flames, but pretty much every other house around them had burned to the ground and was still smoldering. The once magnificent forest that had surrounded the town was now ash.

Faussett admitted that he doesn't understand the buzz about the Kirtland's warbler. With so many other species of warbler around, he doesn't understand why people are so dedicated to this one. He added that in all of his and Mary Jane's years in the Mack Lake area they have never seen a Kirtland's warbler. "I could care less about the bird. If it was you or the bird, I'd save you," he said.

But Faussett saves his harshest criticism for the Forest Service. Despite a weather forecast that called for high winds, Faussett said that the fire was started for one reason and one reason only: it was on the calendar.

Today Mack Lake is a disjointed community spread along the southwest shore of the lake and up a gentle hill. At times, more wild turkeys wander the streets than people. There's no sign of the fire. There's also no gas station or grocery store or any other retail business. It's a place of dead-end streets and rundown shacks and well-maintained lawns and comfortable wood-frame homes built to withstand the harsh winters. On the east edge of town is a thick stand of tall jack pines. In front of the stand is a beat-up wooden sign that reads, "This is Kirtlandia." If the sign was put up as a sarcastic joke after the fire, its meaning is now lost. Most of the town's current residents have moved in over the past ten years. Ask them about the fire, and they will tell you that they've heard about it and shrug.

Although Bill Irvine was in charge of planning for the May 5 prescribed burn, he was not scheduled to participate in it. On the day of the fire, Irvine was in western Michigan to conduct a helicopter-based survey of another threatened bird species, the sandhill crane. Irvine recalls that he was in Manistee when word came over his walkie-talkie late that afternoon that the fire was out of control and the helicopter was needed in Mio as soon as possible. He also heard that one of his coworkers had been killed but didn't find out until later that day that it was Swiderski.

"I knew him well," Irvine said. "He was a good kid. It really hit me hard. I've never really gotten over it."

Irvine admits that Forest Service personnel overseeing the prescribed burn made poor decisions: "If I had been there, it might have been different. I don't know . . ."

The aftermath of the Mack Lake fire provided more questions than answers. While the Forest Service was asking what went wrong and area residents wondered how they would recover, birders and wildlife biologists wanted to know just one thing: What did this disaster mean for the future of the Kirtland's warbler? The fire charred some forty square miles, including prime nesting habitat that likely would have been occupied by warblers when the first birds returned to the area from the Bahamas in just a matter of hours.

Sylvia Taylor, the endangered species coordinator for the Michigan

Department of Natural Resources at the time, looked at the Mack Lake tragedy and saw an opportunity. Taylor was a botanist by training and had a hunch that the Mack Lake fire was a chance to study the Kirtland's warbler's ecosystem in a radically different way. Taylor believed that many of the wildlife biologists who were making decisions about the bird viewed the jack pine ecosystem too narrowly. She also knew exactly who to call: her old colleague at the University of Michigan, Burton Barnes.

Barnes was among the first researchers in North America to look at the natural world in a radical new way. Instead of examining a relationship between two organisms—like the Kirtland's warbler and the jack pine—Barnes would take a more holistic approach, examining the warbler's relationship with all the plants, the topography, the soil, and the climate. The process that Barnes would apply had been developed in Europe to better understand how humans had changed the landscape and how the landscape could be restored to a more natural state.

Barnes and his students first began to study the area just a few days after the fire. Before long, he noticed that the fire had spread across a jack pine forest that grew at three different levels. The lowest level was a series of sixty- to seventy-foot-deep depressions created more than ten thousand years earlier by large "kettles" of ice. The middle level was a vast expanse of jack pine forest. The highest altitude of jack pine abutted the hardwoods growing on glacial moraines. This highest level immediately intrigued Barnes. Even though this level had a sandy, quick-draining soil, it was not the Grayling sand soil that was believed to be so important to the Kirtland's warbler. Barnes believed that the warbler would settle into this higher-elevation habitat first because its warmer, faster-growing habitat would recover more quickly than the colder, slower-growing lowland habitats. Barnes also recognized that this multilevel area had another benefit: because there were multiple microclimates that caused plants to grow faster or slower, the area of the Mack Lake fire would support nesting Kirtland's warblers for a longer time period than if it contained just one ecosystem. By the time the quicker-growing habitat would be getting too old to support nesting, the slowest-growing nesting habitat would be coming into its prime. In this way, the area of the fire would end up supporting the

Kirtland's nesting needs for much longer than an area that foresters typically prepared on a flat outwash plain.

Wildlife biologists were immediately skeptical. The warbler had never been found nesting on anything other than Grayling sand soil. Why would it now nest in a slightly different ecosystem that contained considerably more oaks and fewer jack pines? Barnes, however, was right, and the first Kirtland's warblers began nesting in this higher-level habitat in 1986.

Besides skepticism, Barnes encountered another obstacle to his research. In an effort to protect the nesting warblers, the Michigan Department of Natural Resources blocked Barnes's access to the nesting habitat. For the first year of his study, Barnes was allowed only to work along the edge of the roads that ran through the burn area.

Yes, some DNR wildlife biologists were *that* protective of the Kirtland's warbler. On one occasion they blindfolded a student working a seasonal job for the U.S. Forest Service before leading her to a nest to ensure that she would be unable to find her way back to it if she had secretly intended to return on her own. They didn't want to risk losing even one warbler.

"There were people out there who were extremely conservative— they wouldn't even allow a photographer in," says Bob Hess, former endangered species coordinator for the Michigan DNR. "They would have rather err on the side of the species than think about what might help in the long term."

The DNR, however, relented the following year when a team of research biologists from the U.S. Geological Survey showed up with the intent of working in the area. With the Kirtland's warbler's future still in doubt, Harold Mayfield stepped in and persuaded the DNR that it was time to allow researchers to actively work with the birds. Hesitantly, the DNR relented, and the researchers were allowed in.

Barnes's work was part of a paradigm shift in thinking about the Kirtland's warbler in particular and the jack pine forest in general. Biologists and foresters were no longer making decisions based exclusively on the endangered warbler. Now they were managing the ecosystem based on knowledge of all the plants and animals and soil it contained. And decisions were now being made that were taking the black-backed woodpecker, upland sandpiper, and plants like Hill's thistle and the prairie dandelion into consideration. This shift in thinking had a secondary benefit. When skeptical taxpayers asked why the government was spending so much money and effort on one bird, habitat managers could say that they weren't spending money on just one bird; they were spending it on an entire ecosystem.

In 1986, Barnes and his graduate students started work in a new study area, the Bald Hill section of Camp Grayling, a sprawling Michigan National Guard base, which contains some of the best Kirtland's warbler nesting areas in the state. (Much of Walkinshaw's fieldwork and banding in the 1960s and 1970s took place on the tank range as he regularly found warbler nests built in depressions left by tank treads.)

The Bald Hill fire started on May 10, 1975, as a result of artillery practice. The fire quickly spread beyond the grounds of the military reservation. Even though it burned an area smaller than that of the Mack Lake fire, the result was similar: a multitiered habitat that attracted and maintained Kirtland's warblers for a longer period. Today hardly anyone remembers the Bald Hill fire or the Muskrat Lake fire or the Stephan Bridge Road fire or any of the other innumerable fires that have swept through the jack pines in the past fifty years. But many people remember the Mack Lake fire. And they remember it for two reasons. First, a firefighter was killed. Second, it was set for a bird.

Animosity lingered in the community for years. Even though the Michigan Department of Natural Resources had nothing to do with the fire, that agency could not escape the wrath. Workers reported that angry citizens threw objects at their trucks when they drove through the area. As a result of the community anger immediately after the fire, Forest Service employees were told not to wear their uniforms when they went into town.

The Mack Lake fire was unquestionably a setback in efforts to manage jack pine forests for the Kirtland's warbler. The Forest Service immediately put a halt to all burning as the policies were reviewed and employees given additional training. The fire resulted in a policy change: safety precautions would now become mandatory, and no fire would be started anywhere in the United States unless the rules set by the agency were strictly followed. Even though the fire's death toll officially stands at one, it's not a stretch to say that it would later claim a second victim. Vendel Bosman, the Forest Service's district ranger for Mio and the man who ultimately gave the approval to light the fire, died just about a year after the Mack Lake fire. Friends, family, and coworkers, including Bill Irvine, all wonder if Bosman's death was caused by the sense of responsibility he felt for giving the go-ahead to start the fire.

The Mack Lake Fire cost the U.S. government five million dollars in fire-fighting costs, damage, and claims. The fire burned more than twenty-thousand acres, destroyed forty-four buildings, and released an esti-mated three trillion British thermal units (Btus) of energy—as much as ninety thunderstorms or nine times the energy of the atomic bomb dropped on Hiroshima, Japan, at the end of World War II.[15] Nearly everything in the community of Mack Lake burned down, including the community's fire station. The fire was so hot that it melted one Mack Lake resident's motorcycle into a puddle of metal.

But the impact of the Mack Lake fire on the Kirtland's warbler pop-ulation would also be dramatic. It would produce ten thousand acres of prime nesting habitat, which nearly tripled the amount available. In 1986, the first year in which warblers would occupy the burn area, the annual census found 210 singing males. Ten years later, the 1996 census found 692 singing males. Over that ten-year period, nearly 70 percent of the nesting population of the Kirtland's warbler would be found in the area of the Mack Lake burn. The fire, combined with a new Kirtland's warbler management plan, which created massive new jack pine plantations and nesting habitat, ensured ample habitat well into the future.

There is no doubt in the mind of the DNR's Weinrich that the acci-dent at Bald Hill and the tragedy at Mack Lake saved the Kirtland's warbler from extinction. "Mack Lake was a disaster in lots of ways," he said, "but it came along at the right time."

SIX : A Working Landscape

In the immediate aftermath of the Mack Lake fire, the attitudes of many Mio area residents turned against the Forest Service. Death threats were made against employees, and on one occasion the lug nuts on a front wheel of one Forest Service vehicle were loosened, causing the wheel to fall off as a crew was driving it on a highway. Luckily, no one was hurt.

Besides setting their anger loose on government employees, locals also turned against the Kirtland's warbler—a bird most people knew little about but up until then had been a source of local pride. Residents no longer referred to the Kirtland's warbler by name. It was now known as "that damn bird."

In the taverns and stores of Mio, anti–Kirtland's warbler petitions were circulated and "wanted" posters went up. One of the posters hung up around town featured a photo of a bird covered by a red circle with a slash. As if to emphasize that the residents didn't fully understand why they were angry, the bird pictured on the poster was a female black-throated blue warbler.

By the late 1980s, even though nearly a decade had passed since the Mack Lake fire, animosity toward the Forest Service and the Michigan Department of Natural Resources remained high. But now it wasn't just about Mack Lake. Mio area residents had a growing list of complaints. Even though the use of prescribed burns had ended, people couldn't understand why beautiful forests were being replaced with ugly clear-cuts. Local businesspeople grumbled that the warbler was

77

a hindrance to growth because so much land was set aside for the bird while others claimed tourists and hunters did not want to come to an area of northern Michigan that didn't have mature forests. Some hunters argued that the clear-cutting was harming white-tailed deer, wild turkey, and snowshoe hare populations. Mushroom hunters and hikers complained that vast areas of Kirtland's warbler nesting habitat were closed to their activities. Pressure was growing on the keepers of the Kirtland's, and they needed to act quickly to persuade area residents to be more tolerant of their small but demanding neighbor.

It was time to sell the Kirtland's warbler.

Rex Ennis, a district wildlife biologist with the U.S. Forest Service, was excited about transferring to Mio in 1988 from his job in the Mark Twain National Forest in southern Missouri. Ennis was looking to advance his career within the agency when a job as forest wildlife biologist in the Huron-Manistee National Forests came open. In this job, Ennis would become administrator of the forests' wildlife and rare resource program and be responsible for all the wildlife within the forests' boundaries. Although he knew of the situation in Mio—the public's anger toward the agency and the warbler—he never gave it a second thought. Ennis already knew and liked several of the Forest Service people who worked in Mio and was eager to work with the Kirtland's Warbler Recovery Team.

But once Ennis arrived in Mio, it didn't take long for him to realize that perhaps the most pressing task of the recovery team had nothing to do with the bird itself.

Bob Hess, a wildlife biologist with the Michigan Department of Natural Resources who had been working with the Kirtland's warbler for several years, had already reached the same conclusion. Hess had been the endangered species coordinator for the state of Michigan in Lansing before transferring to Mio to work in the field. In both Lansing and Mio, Hess had been getting an earful for nearly a decade. He later recalled, "There was a feeling locally that all this land was being set aside for the Kirtland's warbler and they [the residents] said that if you took all the Kirtland's warblers and put them in one spot, they wouldn't fill a bushel basket. . . . They couldn't figure out why we put all this land aside for one dinky bird."

But Hess wasn't just hearing it from the general public, as some of Hess's colleagues inside the DNR were making it clear that they did not care for the way the Kirtland's warbler recovery efforts were receiving so much money and attention. Many of the old-guard game biologists wondered why so much effort was being put into something that couldn't be hunted. With jack pine having so little economic value, DNR foresters argued that more resources should be put into timber with more value. At least that was the argument they made. The foresters' unspoken objection to Kirtland's warbler management was that they did not like being told what to plant and how to plant it by wildlife biologists.

Based on what they were hearing, Hess, Ennis, and other members of the recovery team recognized that there were many misconceptions not just about the Kirtland's warbler but also about the recovery effort. The best way to change attitudes, they began to conclude, would be to create an outreach program that would help local residents understand the habitat's value to the Kirtland's warbler and the Kirtland's warbler's value to the region.

But Hess and Ennis realized that they were biologists and didn't know much about public relations. Hess, however, did know someone he thought could help. In a different job a few years earlier, Hess had worked with David Case, the president of D. J. Case and Associates, an Indiana-based public relations firm. Together, Hess and Case had created an educational program for the check box on the state income tax form that allowed taxpayers to voluntarily donate a portion of their income tax refund to support endangered wildlife. Hess was impressed with the company's work on the campaign and guessed that Case would be up for this new but very different challenge.

Case jumped at the opportunity. He was already familiar with the Kirtland's warbler from his days in college, and coincidentally he had started his master's degree fieldwork on North Manitou Island in Lake Michigan just a few days after the Mack Lake fire. Facing the real world after completing his master's degree, Case discovered there were no jobs in the Michigan Department of Natural Resources and turned his attention to finding one out of state. In 1983 he took a job as an information specialist with the Kansas Wildlife and Parks Department. A master's degree in wildlife ecology from the University of Michigan did not prepare him to write press releases and develop public relations campaigns, so he returned to the classroom. Between the classroom and his job, it didn't take long for Case to realize that there was opportunity for him in this field, and in 1986 he left the state job to form his own communications firm.

At the time, Case saw that even though environmentalists and state and federal natural resource management agencies were doing good work, they often did a poor job of explaining what they were doing or why they were doing it. That gap often led members of the general public to misunderstand and mistrust environmental organizations, even if they were sympathetic toward their missions. Case started his firm with the goal of being able to enhance communication among the general public, government agencies, and nongovernmental conservation groups. He took on the project from the Kirtland's Warbler Recovery Team determined to close the gap in Mio.

Before Case could develop an educational program, he needed to understand what people knew about the Kirtland's warbler. So he immediately set about developing a list of names of stakeholders—officials in county government, members of the local chambers of commerce, conservation groups, representatives of the timber industry, and citizens who had expressed opposition to the bird—and made appointments not to lecture but to ask questions, listen to concerns, and ultimately understand.

After months of interviews and several trips to northern Michigan, Case shared his findings with the Kirtland's Warbler Recovery Team in December 1991. The survey was revealing. Yes, there was suspicion of the government's habitat work, but it was because the citizens didn't understand that the Kirtland's warbler regularly needed new habitat in order to nest. He told the recovery team that hunters didn't like the warbler because they thought its nesting areas were off-limits year-round, not just for a few months in the summer. And, more than

anything else, he told them that local residents feared another govern-
ment-set wildfire.

Case issued a series of recommendations that were all rooted in
one goal: help Mio area residents see the value of living so close to the
Kirtland's warbler. His recommendations were as follows.

> The agencies should establish regular communications with area
> residents. Agency people needed to take time to communicate
> one-on-one with people in the community on a casual basis,
> but they also needed to establish formal channels with local
> elected officials and community leaders. He suggested that
> agency employees should invite local officials and VIPs to go
> out and view Kirtland's warblers on an ongoing basis.
>
> The agencies should create a fire education program to help
> people living in jack pine areas understand how they can
> protect their homes from wildfire. Modern fire suppression
> had given many area residents a false sense of security when
> it came to living in the jack pine, even though the risk of fire
> remained high.
>
> Brochures, pamphlets, press releases, and videos should be
> targeted toward different audiences. It was clear to Case that
> different groups of people needed different kinds of informa-
> tion. He recommended that the bird's historical connection
> with fire be explained but also suggested that the materials
> should stay clear of any discussion of prescribed burns to avoid
> opening old wounds.
>
> Educational materials should be developed for use in Michigan's
> elementary schools.
>
> Signs should be placed along clear-cuts to help explain why large
> tracts had been cut and replanted.
>
> The agencies should acknowledge and be honest about the Mack
> Lake fire.
>
> The Kirtland's warbler should be used as a tool to help people
> understand the importance of the overall jack pine ecosystem
> to wildlife, neotropical birds, and biodiversity.

Case also recommended that the team take the communications effort beyond Mio and tell the Kirtland's warbler recovery story to forestry organizations, environmental groups, civic clubs, and churches across Michigan and the nation. At every meeting, the presenter should be sure to leave time to answer questions and accept feedback.

Case concluded that if the agencies did a better job of sharing information, local residents would not only begin to understand jack pine management but they would be willing to work with the agencies to solve problems.

Finally, he said that the agencies needed to get residents to understand that the Kirtland's warblers nest on "a working landscape"—an area that requires extensive and ongoing intervention, cultivation, and renewal. Between the lines, Case could well have been referring to the relationship between the agencies and the local citizenry. It, too, was a working landscape, and it had been neglected for too long.

Before members of the recovery team could develop and implement Case's plan, however, they got a slap in the face on May 28, 1991, when state representative Thomas Hickner, a Democrat from Bay City, introduced a resolution in the Michigan House of Representatives that called for a total reexamination of the Kirtland's warbler management plan. Hickner introduced the resolution on behalf of a group of his central Michigan constituents who were summer residents of Crawford County and were upset with recent DNR clear-cuts on behalf of the Kirtland's warbler. Even though the measure was just a resolution and would not have the force of law, it was a further reminder that the recovery team had lost control of the message.

The mere fact that this resolution was introduced was insulting to some members of the recovery team. It was rife with misinformation and false assumptions even though Hickner was a member of the House Conservation, Recreation, and Environment Committee. Among other things, the resolution claimed that the Kirtland's warbler management plan would "create a forest which is basically unsuited to the needs of most wildlife presently indigenous to the area," implying that the DNR could or should be planting white pines and hardwoods in the nutrient-poor sandy soils of the barrens.

The resolution went on to call for the immediate cessation of clear-cutting under the Kirtland's warbler management plan, requested a scientific reevaluation of the plan and a survey to determine the impact of clear-cutting on wildlife, and the establishment of a citizens advisory committee to provide input in the development of a new policy—presumably one that did not involve clear-cutting.

An immediate cessation of clear-cutting? If the Mack Lake fire took prescribed burning out of the foresters' tool kit, the only tool they had left was clear-cutting. There was no other option other than allowing the forest to mature and die. Besides, the DNR's clear-cuts were doing residents of the area a favor because the harvests were reducing the chance of another devastating wildfire.

A scientific reevaluation of the Kirtland's warbler management plan? Even though there was a growing body of science on the Kirtland's warbler's jack pine ecosystem, the recovery team and its agencies were already using the best available science to guide their decisions.

Many members of the recovery team were dumbfounded by the resolution, and some even considered it a slap. Despite the perceived slight, the DNR immediately moved to set up a town hall meeting with local homeowners and summer residents to explain Kirtland's warbler management. Shortly before the meeting was to be held, however, the residents canceled it without giving a reason. At the same time, Hickner's resolution was well on its way to dying in committee.

In the end, the resolution amounted to nothing. Nevertheless, it reminded the recovery team that it had lost control of the message, and its members moved quickly to implement Case's education plan.

Adopting Case's recommendations meant a significant change in culture for the Kirtland's Warbler Recovery Team and its member agencies because it was no longer just about the bird. Team members developed new communications that deemphasized the Kirtland's warbler and put the focus on the importance of the jack pine habitat. They created a video that explained the importance of the jack pine habitat to the Kirtland's warbler and other wildlife and the traditional role that fire has had in the habitat. They developed a drivable self-guided wildlife viewing tour with signage that explained the overall importance of jack pine habitat and acknowledged the tragedy of the

Mack Lake fire. They developed a fire education program for residents of the jack pine region, which recommended that expansive lawns be planted as firebreaks between the forest and structures. But perhaps the most important change came in the way the recovery team conducted its business. Now public education would be a regular agenda topic at team meetings, and the retrenchment that came in the wake of the Mack Lake fire would be replaced with a strategy of engagement.

As part of that strategy of engagement, Case considered recommending the creation of an annual Kirtland's warbler festival in Mio but did not include the recommendation in his final report because, in the end, he concluded that Mio was too small and lacked the resources to organize a sizable festival. In 1994, however, he was pleasantly proven wrong. Not only did Mio hold a festival, but its impact was felt well beyond the jack pine.

Tourism isn't exactly a booming business in northeastern lower Michigan. The Au Sable River attracts canoeists and anglers, and trails through the Huron National Forest bring in hikers and off-road vehicles. But for many of Michigan's tourists, Mio is an area to drive past to get to resorts or cottages or chic-boutique towns on the coast of one of the Great Lakes. Frustrated with watching the dollars drive by, the Mio Chamber of Commerce in the early 1990s held a brainstorming session to think of ways to attract new tourism to the area.

Vergie Purchase, who owned Mio Acres Campground with her husband, Richard, suggested that the town start a festival for the warbler. If there are festivals to celebrate fish and flowers, Purchase said, Mio should be able to celebrate the arrival of the Kirtland's warbler on its nesting grounds. With help from her husband and their two children, Purchase sent invitations to officials in Lansing and Washington. Vice President Al Gore declined the invitation to visit, but Interior Secretary Bruce Babbitt quickly accepted—raising the stakes for festival organizers. Local agency people were both thrilled and intimidated by the prospect of Babbitt's visit and quickly pledged their help. With an important official coming from Washington, local politicians also pledged their support, and Oscoda County volunteered the lawn of the county courthouse for the festival site. Still short on manpower, organizers partnered with a local group of iris enthusiasts who already had a well-established springtime festival, which meant this would be an iris and Kirtland's warbler festival in 1994.

On the day of the festival, Babbitt toured Kirtland's warbler nesting grounds and a banding station with an entourage of reporters and was thrilled when a Kirtland's warbler, curious about the intruders in his territory, landed on the ground just a few feet away from him.

Babbitt came away from his northern Michigan trip impressed. In Mio, he saw a community that was ready and willing to work with the government to preserve a bird and its habitat. Babbitt expressed his pleasure in a guest column in *Defenders,* the magazine of the Defenders of Wildlife. He wrote that he believed that Mio had taken the right approach to preserving endangered species while protecting private property rights and recreational opportunities. This, Babbitt argued, was a model for endangered species protection for the rest of the country.

> The Mio model is one that offers hope that we can learn to use the Endangered Species Act as a tool for conservation consonant with the needs of local economies and private landowners. In the short time since President Bill Clinton took office, we've seen some other important habitat conservation models that, like the story of the Kirtland's warbler, show how property owners and government can work together both to protect endangered species and to sustain economic development. . . . As stewards of this planet, we have witnessed the demise of countless species. Our own country has already lost such fabled species as the passenger pigeon and the Carolina parakeet. Protecting biodiversity is a worldwide issue, but the job begins at home. We cannot hope to save tigers and rhinos beyond our borders unless we can demonstrate the wherewithal and creativity to conserve habitat in our own backyard. Mio, Michigan, is calling out to all of us to replicate its example.[1]

Had Mio become a model for the rest of the nation? Had things improved that dramatically in just three years? Or was Mio a Potemkin village with residents demonstrating their midwestern hospitality by biting their tongues for a day? Looking back, agency people attending that first festival report a mixed message. There is no question that the festival was poorly attended. In fact, agency employees standing around with their hands in their pockets outnumbered the general public. But if Babbitt's attendance and the recognition that came with it didn't impress the citizens of Mio, it went a long way toward boosting the morale of those agency people who had been working hard on the conservation of the Kirtland's warbler.

"His visit reaffirmed that what we were doing was a good thing and it was the right thing to do," said Phil Huber, a wildlife biologist with the U.S. Forest Service. "And to have him cite us as a model program—that was a pretty special thing."

Even though the initial festival was poorly attended, it represented a turning point. In just three years it outgrew the courthouse lawn in Mio. The Michigan Department of Natural Resources approached Kirtland Community College, and the school's president immediately agreed to take over the festival. With its additional manpower, resources, and reach throughout northeastern Michigan, the college has built the festival into an annual event that hosts visitors from around the world and is attended by more than fifteen hundred people annually.

It's just before 8:00 a.m. on a mid-May Saturday morning, and the campus of Kirtland Community College is unusually active for a weekend. The sun is out, but it's chilly and there is a bit of a breeze, so the few people who are out and moving clutch their coffee mugs to keep their hands warm. Local craftspeople and merchants unload their minivans and pickups, set up tents, and stock their tables with products that range from homemade birdhouses to tote bags. Next to the merchants is a tent where stacks of precut wood wait for children to assemble them into birdhouses. Next to that tent is a petting zoo, where wallabies, a zebra, and a couple of llamas wait to be poked and prodded by curious children. Near the petting zoo is a trailer containing a reptile display, including a six-foot-long alligator and three of Africa's most poisonous snakes. All this seemingly unrelated stuff is here because it's the third Saturday in May and time for the annual Kirtland's Warbler Wildlife Festival.

Nearby, more than fifty bird-watchers are gathered, quietly milling about outside the main festival tent. They are a mix of little old ladies in sweatshirts and tennis shoes and hardcore birders carrying high-powered viewing scopes and wearing caps bearing logos from well-known North American birding hot spots or the brand names of cameras and binoculars. They are a mix of local residents, people who have driven up from the Detroit area, and visitors from as far away as North Carolina, Colorado, Washington, and the United Kingdom.

Two yellow school buses pull up, and everyone eagerly climbs aboard. Even though the birders are now out of the chill, there's very little chatter, that is until Mike Petrucha gets on the bus. Petrucha, a wildlife assistant with the DNR, will act as field guide, encyclopedia, and master of ceremonies for this bus. He's a bear of a man with a ragged salt-and-pepper beard, long hair stuffed under a faded cap, and a resemblance to Rubeus Hagrid of the Harry Potter movies. Petrucha's lyrical voice and offbeat, irreverent sense of humor immediately put the birders at ease, and he buoys spirits when he guarantees that everyone on the bus will see at least a pair of Kirtland's warblers this morning. What Petrucha doesn't tell them is that he has a backup plan. If the group is unable to find warblers in the jack pine this morning, he will pull up his pant leg to expose the pair of them tattooed on the inside of his right calf.

Petrucha has worked on behalf of the Kirtland's warbler since 1990, which is when he was hired by the U.S. Fish and Wildlife Service to coordinate cowbird trapping. Even though he worked for the DNR as a wildlife assistant in southern lower Michigan, he attended the festival as a volunteer. "Pretty much any of the warbler stuff I do is volunteer," he said. Because of Michigan's declining tax base and the DNR's shrinking budget, Petrucha usually needs to use vacation time to attend the twice-yearly meetings of the Kirtland's Warbler Recovery Team or help with the census in June. He is philosophical when talking about what he's able to do on behalf of the Kirtland's warbler, but the irony of using vacation time to do volunteer work for his employer is not lost on him.

The two buses pull out of the campus onto the county highway and almost immediately make a right turn onto a sandy road that takes them into a stand of mature red pine. Tree branches scrape against the sides of the buses, and everybody on board bounces up and down with every pothole. The buses head into extreme northwestern Ogemaw County, a location Petrucha knows as 24N, 1E. It's a tract of land in the Au Sable State Forest that he's visited several times.

After just a couple of miles, the buses leave the tall red pines and enter a vast area of small scrubby trees. "Right now," he announces to the bus, "we're in occupied habitat."

Faces turn to the windows. The buses take one more right-hand turn and come to a halt. Stepping off the buses, the group is met immediately with an assortment of birdsongs—and a stiff breeze. One is a good sign because it means the birds are active. The other one is not, because the wind will cause the birds to stay low in the trees, and that will inhibit the group's ability to see them. Either way, Petrucha is grateful that it's not snowing. (Even though it is mid-May, it snowed during a previous festival.) It takes only a few seconds for Petrucha's experienced ear to sort through the songs of hermit thrushes and Lincoln's sparrows to isolate the song of a Kirtland's warbler and point the birders in that direction.

This is classic Kirtland's warbler habitat—short, scrubby pines and taller dead oaks—and it stretches for miles. The birders tentatively make their way over the rough ground, around foot-tall anthills, through willow and cherry scrub, and over charred tree limbs and trunks to the edge of a stand of five-foot-tall jack pines.

As if on cue, a male Kirtland's warbler pops up and lands on a bare branch of a deciduous tree that is a good three feet taller than the surrounding pine. It sits for a couple of seconds, sings once, and dives back toward the ground. Members of the group squeal with delight at seeing the bird and groan with disappointment when it disappears so quickly. Over the next half hour, the bird pops up every few minutes as it works its way counterclockwise around an area the size of a football field. The singing is constant, however, and it's easy to follow its progress. There is a lot of standing around, waiting for glimpses that last just for a few seconds, but the weather is warming and everyone is entranced.

After about an hour of following the male Kirtland's around his territory, everyone files back on the bus and heads off for a cowbird trap for a short presentation on the dark side of Kirtland's warbler habitat management. From there it's back to campus, where the festival is now in full swing.

The smell of charcoal and grilling chicken provides a fitting transition from early morning to the approaching lunch for the birders as they step off the bus. Over at the kids' tent, it's nearly impossible to hold a conversation over the sound of children hammering together their birdhouses. At a pond near the entrance to the campus, other children excitedly cast for trout. Over at the campus's art museum, just a bit of a walk south of the main campus, there is a reception for a juried nature art show, and student entries for the annual Kirtland's warbler calendar contest are on display. Inside the Student Center, there are displays of works by a nature photographer and nature artist. The Michigan Audubon Society has stocked several tables with nature books for sale. A representative of the U.S. Postal Service sells commemorative stamps and offers special Kirtland's Warbler Wildlife Festival cancellations for letters and postcards. In a room off to the side, members of a local gem and mineral club teach children how to polish stones. There's also an area where a local bird rehabilitation organization has injured hawks and owls on display. In various other rooms around campus there are presentations on wildflowers, insects, fish, and other animals. The festival's featured presentation on the Kirtland's warbler is held in the auditorium. There, only a few people—most of them from the morning's field trip—listen to experts from the U.S. Fish and Wildlife Service, the U.S. Forest Service, and the Michigan Department of Natural Resources describe the Kirtland's warbler's battle for survival.

Kirtland Community College took over the festival in 1997, and the event has steadily grown under the guidance of the college's director of marketing, Jim Enger.

Enger's kingdom for the day is the main festival tent, where he greets visitors and chats with friends. This is where the official Kirtland's Warbler Festival hats, T-shirts, calendars, and postcards are for sale. Noticeably missing from the items for sale are tacky tchotchkes—Kirtland's warbler figurines with anthropomorphized features, plush toys, or shot glasses. It's indicative of Enger's goal for the festival: quality education, quality family fun, and quality merchandise.

Enger stresses that the daylong festival is only one small part of the college's efforts to help the bird and the community. In the week prior to the festival, the college brings in natural science educators from around the country to work with students. And in the two months prior to the festival, Tom Dale, a retired biology instructor, gives a presentation on the jack pine habitat to students from nearly every elementary and middle school in the area.

Enger says that, yes, this is a "Kirtland's warbler festival," but it's also a family-friendly nature festival intended to serve the local community, and that helps to explain the frantic birdhouse construction and the presence of a six-foot gator.

Still, the focus is on the bird and connecting people with it either by helping them understand its importance or helping them see it for the first time. Enger is thrilled when he hears people talk about seeing the warbler. One of his favorite memories is of three men who flew from San Diego to Chicago the day before the festival, arriving around midnight. At the airport, they rented a car and drove all night to campus, arriving just in time for the 7:00 a.m. tour. "I happened to be there when the bus got back [from the tour]," he said, "and they were smiling from ear to ear. You would have thought they had won the World Series of Birding. Their goal was to see the Kirtland's warbler, and they did it. And they all had excellent sightings. That's not untypical of the kind of people who are on this tour. They're enthusiastic birders."

Once the Kirtland's warbler tours are over, the hard-core birders tend to drift off, leaving the festival grounds to locals who are there to build birdhouses, climb on camels, stare at snakes, and gape at gators.

As a result of the festival and the education effort, there was a noticeable change in attitudes. Not only was there a feeling among agency people that their relationship with the public was improving, but the change was documented by a 1997 study. That study reported that of those respondents who gave an opinion about local attitudes toward the Kirtland's warbler, 83 percent thought attitudes had become more positive specifically as a result of the festival.[2]

Without question, Bob Hess of the DNR credits the festival. "It was helpful for members of the community to see us as real people and not just bureaucrats," he said.

In addition to the festival, recovery team members were seeing results from Case's plan. By the time Case returned in 1998 to evaluate the implementation of his plan, the recovery team had met more than 80 percent of its goals. Case lauded the creation of the self-guided driving tour, communications efforts, and the development of brochures, posters, and two booklets for Mio area residents, *Your Neighbor, the Kirtland's Warbler* and *Working Together to Save a Special Bird*.

Furthermore, Hess says, the effort to educate people about the dangers of fire had been taken to heart by area residents. Jack pine trees had been cut away from people's homes, replaced with lawns that act as a fire buffer. Today there are fire officers in each Kirtland's warbler management area who talk to schools and civic organizations and train local firefighters.

Case's plan gave the recovery team a road map, but Rex Ennis says that nothing would have improved if the team had botched its implementation by arguing over costs or responsibilities or trying too hard to sell the Kirtland's warbler. Instead, the outreach process was a collaborative effort, with each agency contributing funding, time, and manpower. Ennis also says that even though the recovery team and individual agencies were "selling" the Kirtland's warbler, it was a soft sell. It was important that local residents discovered the importance of the warbler on their own, because any hard sell likely would have been rejected by an already suspicious population.

With visitors coming from around the world to attend the festival and see the Kirtland's warbler, residents of Mio, Grayling, and Roscommon were beginning to understand the financial impact it was having on their region.

Mike DeCapita, a retired wildlife biologist from the U.S. Fish and Wildlife Service, says he will never forget the reaction of hotel employees in Grayling after they booked four people from France who were coming for the Kirtland's warbler tour. DeCapita said he understood early in his career that people from around the world would want to see the bird, but he often struggled to get local residents to understand this opportunity.

For example, when the Fish and Wildlife Service needed a new location for the Kirtland's warbler tours in the late 1980s, DeCapita initially approached the city of Grayling to see about using an empty room in the city building. When DeCapita was rebuffed by the city, some DNR employees suggested the tours be anchored at the local Holiday Inn (now a Ramada Inn). The inn's owner and staff quickly saw an opportunity for some added business and offered a room at no cost to taxpayers in exchange for the opportunity to market the facility to the tourists. The Fish and Wildlife Service tours have operated out of that motel ever since, and it hosts hundreds of Kirtland's warbler tourists every spring and summer.

Of course, tourists need souvenirs, and down a side street in Grayling is Au Sable Gifts, a shop filled with moccasins, fleece jackets, and T-shirts that reflect the northern Michigan attitude and lifestyle. The shop's owner, Kris Madill, devotes one small corner of her shop to the Kirtland's warbler, offering refrigerator magnets, hats, T-shirts, postcards, and pins. Madill sells out of most of her Kirtland's warbler merchandise every year.

Despite people coming from all over the world to see the Kirtland's warbler, its direct economic impact remains small. A 2005 survey by Larry Leefers, a forestry professor at Michigan State University, found that more than two thousand unique visitors come to the region annually just to see the Kirtland's warbler. The economic value of those visits equaled the creation of two jobs.[3]

Still, the people of northern lower Michigan are now recognizing the value of the Kirtland's warbler, and Case's plan appears to have worked. With attitudes toward the warbler changed and tensions dispelled, agency people have finally exhaled. But despite the change in attitude, there is one thing that agency employees know has not changed, and no educational or public relations plan will likely ever make a difference: area residents still live in fear of another Mack Lake–style fire and probably will forever.

SEVEN : An Unseasoned Challenger
Takes on the Incumbent

As bills in the Michigan Legislature go, S.B. 740 of 2003 was unusually short, simple and straightforward. The entire proposal—just 12
words—read: "The Kirtland's warbler (Dendroica kirtlandii) is the
official bird of this state." The measure was introduced by state senator
Patricia Birkholz, a warm, grandmotherly Republican from Saugatuck.

But after newspapers began to write about Birkholz's bill, a few
calls and letters in opposition trickled in to legislators. Some citizens
supported keeping the American robin as the state bird. Other citizens agreed that the robin needed to go, but they would rather see
it replaced with the black-capped chickadee, a friendly year-round
resident familiar to every Michigander. Still others wondered why the
legislators were wasting time on this issue when the state was facing
a 920 million dollar budget deficit, corporate downsizing, increasing
unemployment, and people moving out of the state in droves.

But Birkholz had a comeback: this issue was important because
technically Michigan did not have a state bird. In 1931, the robin was
declared the state bird by *resolution*, not law, and resolutions are in
force only as long as that particular session of the Legislature is sitting.
Even though the robin appears on the state's official road map and in
other official documents, it only holds the honor through tradition.

Birkholz was not the first person to propose the Kirtland's warbler
for state bird. The Michigan Audubon Society proposed giving the title
to the Kirtland's warbler in 1929, jumping on a national trend of nam-
ing state birds. The idea went nowhere in the Legislature, as there was

little support for such an obscure bird. With the warbler a nonstarter, the Audubon Society organized a statewide vote by schoolchildren. Eventually, more than two hundred thousand votes were cast by the children, with the robin barely nosing—or beaking—out the chickadee. The Kirtland's warbler didn't get a single vote; it wasn't even on the ballot.

Based solely on that poll of kids, the state House of Representatives approved Concurrent Resolution 30 of 1931, which designated the robin as Michigan's state bird because it was "the best known and best loved of all the birds in the State of Michigan." It was best loved by the children, perhaps, but not by Michigan Audubon Society president Edith Munger, who, shortly after the resolution was approved, predicted the robin's reign would someday end.

Two attempts—one in the 1960s and one in the 1970s—to have the Kirtland's warbler named state bird failed miserably, and the issue went dormant until 2003, when Len Stuttman, a member of the Capital Area Audubon Society in Lansing, started calling members of the Legislature. Stuttman wasn't interested in denigrating the robin or the black-capped chickadee; he only wanted to offer reasons why the warbler was a better choice.

> The warbler would be unique to Michigan, whereas the state shares the robin with Wisconsin and Connecticut.
>
> The chickadee wouldn't be any better, as it is already the state bird of Massachusetts and Maine.
>
> The warbler's primary nesting site is in Michigan, and thousands of birders come from all over the world each year just to see it.
>
> Why not give Michigan a symbol that is primarily associated with no other state?

About the same time that Stuttman was starting his campaign, Vickie Weiss and her class of third, fourth, and fifth graders at City School in Grand Blanc were starting a lesson on how to write a position paper. Using a curriculum sponsored by the Michigan Department of Natural Resources, Weiss asked her students to take a stand on which bird—the robin or the chickadee—would make a better state bird for Michigan and why. At the time, Weiss didn't count on the emergence of a third bird—one she knew little about and had never seen. But shortly after the students began to research the issue they came across a Michigan Audubon Society website promoting the Kirtland's warbler, and soon they were rallying around the third-party candidate. At the request of the students, Weiss contacted Stuttman. Soon Stuttman and the students would be going to Lansing to testify on behalf of legislation in front of the Senate Committee on Local, Urban, and State Affairs.

Despite getting a committee hearing, Birkholz's proposal was never considered by the full Senate; her bill died in the committee when legislators failed to detect support for the change. Today Stuttman has harsh words for those bird-watchers who did little or nothing to support the change. But Stuttman refuses to give up despite having suffered a stroke in December 2007 that left him slightly paralyzed and unable to speak without a slur. He still has the fire to have the warbler named Michigan's state bird, though now he is looking for someone else to take the lead.

Birkholz, on the other hand, is more inclined to blame the legislative process than any individual. Ultimately, she says, the effort to have the Kirtland's warbler declared the state bird of Michigan failed because it was an election year and lawmakers were unwilling to stick their necks out even for what sounded like a fairly innocuous change.

"There's politics and there's policy," Birkholz says. "And sometimes politics win out."

After the bill died, Birkholz told supporters that she would not push for the Kirtland's warbler again until she was certain she had enough votes to ensure passage. That's because if the bill actually made it all the way to the floor of the House or Senate and was voted down the Legislature would be unwilling to consider it again for many years.

And Michigan is still without an official state bird.

PART TWO : *The Present*

EIGHT : The Science

Sarah Rockwell hunkers down behind a tree, toenail clippers at the ready, waiting for her prey. Her quarry is a male Kirtland's warbler. Rockwell doesn't want to kill the warbler; she merely wants to trim his toenail. And take a little blood and snatch a crown feather, too.

Rockwell, a doctoral candidate at the University of Maryland, is among the hundreds of researchers and private citizens who have come to northern Michigan's jack pine forest over the past fifty years to study or just count the endangered Kirtland's warbler. Although Rockwell is only in the third year of a five-year project, she is the latest researcher whose work has helped to provide information that has been used to prevent the warbler's extinction. With this project, Rockwell is taking Kirtland's warbler research in a new direction; she is looking to tie the winter diet and habitat of a male Kirtland's warbler to its summer nesting success in Michigan. She defines nesting success as the number of offspring a male produces, including his ability to produce a second brood if the first nest is unsuccessful and his ability to attempt a second brood after a successful first one. Rockwell is doing this by analyzing chemical "fingerprints" known as isotopes in the birds' toenails, blood, and feathers and then by correlating the bird's chemical signature with its breeding proficiency. The isotopes Rockwell is studying are incorporated into body tissues during the warblers' seven-month stay in the Bahamas and reflect their diet, habitat, and latitude. Rockwell's research could answer a question that is

Sarah Rockwell, a doctoral student at the University of Maryland, follows a male Kirtland's warbler in hopes he will lead her to his nest. Once Rockwell finds the nest, she and members of her research team will monitor it until the young birds fledge.

critical to the Kirtland's warbler and bird conservation in general: do events on the wintering grounds have a significant effect on occurrences on the nesting grounds?

The answer to that question appears to be yes based on research on American redstarts by Peter Marra of the Smithsonian's Migratory Bird Center. Marra's research showed that in Jamaica redstarts in mangroves maintained better body condition and departed earlier in spring than those in dry scrub habitat just a few miles away on the same island. Marra is also Rockwell's adviser. If Rockwell's work in Michigan can establish a correlation for the Kirtland's warbler, she will be able to provide vital new information about habitats and locations that need to be preserved in the Bahamas.

Rockwell hypothesized that male Kirtland's warblers that winter in wetter habitats in the Bahamas would arrive in Michigan earlier than their counterparts that had wintered in drier areas, but so far her data have failed to confirm her hypothesis. The birds that return to the nesting ground the earliest face significant risks: snow and subfreezing temperatures and a lack of food. But there is also a significant reward: they can claim the best nesting territories and have more time to renest in case of a failure or have a second brood. Perhaps, Rockwell says, birds coming north from higher quality winter habitat can risk an earlier arrival because they are fatter and healthier than their counterparts.

A curious person might wonder two things at this point.

Why not conduct winter habitat research on the birds when they are actually on their winter grounds in the Bahamas?

If the goal is to correlate nesting success with winter habitat, why not take tissue samples from the females since they have a larger impact on nesting success than the males?

First, it's much easier to conduct this research in Michigan than in the Bahamas. During the winter, Kirtland's warblers are generally silent and nearly impossible to find in the dense subtropical foliage of an extensive archipelago. In Michigan, the vast majority of Kirtland's warblers nest in just a few counties in the northern part of Michigan's Lower Peninsula. Look for the warbler in good jack pine nesting habitat in May and June and it's fairly easy to find a male singing loudly from the top of a tree.

Second, Rockwell's team does not work with females because they do not want to be too intrusive during the nesting period. Rockwell is not all that upset about not working with females because by the time nesting begins the birds would have been on the breeding grounds for nearly a month. Tissue samples taken this late would be influenced by their northern Michigan diet and would no longer provide strong winter data. Rockwell could try to target females as they arrive, but she believes the results would be not be worth the effort since females often remain secluded in the undergrowth and generally do not respond to playback of taped songs. Finally, since females are much less conspicuous than males, it's nearly impossible to determine arrival dates with any accuracy. Without accurate arrival dates, Rockwell is not confident that the blood samples from females would be collected quickly enough to provide good winter data.

Rockwell admits that even though nesting success is probably more directly linked to the quality and condition of the female, a healthy male is critical because:

> An early-arriving, high-quality male should be able to attract a high-quality female.
>
> The investment of the male in the entire reproduction process can make a big difference. A male that feeds his mate often while she is incubating reduces the time she is off the nest. A female's time on the nest produces a more consistent egg temperature, which improves the hatching rate.
>
> A male in good condition after migration should be better able to devote more effort to feeding nestlings rather than feeding himself.

The fieldwork in northern Michigan is difficult, repetitive, frustrating, and, yes, fun for Rockwell and the four other members of her team: Alana Demko of Yellowknife, Northwest Territories, Canada; Schuyler Brounce of Pittsburgh, Pennsylvania; Patience Falatek of Patton, Pennsylvania; and Ehren Banfield of Montgomery City, Missouri. The five lived together from May 1 to the end of July in a house near Mio during their one field season as a group. Isolated in northern Michigan, Brounce admits that life can get tedious at times. They watch a lot of movies on DVD and spend time canoeing on a local lake. Their closest Internet connection is in the Mio Public Library. Otherwise, there isn't much to do outside of research. Rockwell is the luckiest of the group; she's from Cadillac, Michigan, a town that's less than two hours away. She can occasionally go home and visit her parents and get a good meal. Although she doesn't want to speak for the other members of her team, she says she loves being "stuck" in northern Michigan for the summer, as she is able to swim, hike, kayak, and mountain bike.

To pass time, the team goes tubing on the Au Sable River, visits the Amish stores and farmers' markets, and has the occasional bonfire. On special occasions the team will drive forty-five minutes to West Branch to visit the Dairy Queen and a movie theater.

"If we didn't have to get up at 5:00 a.m., it would be a lot like summer camp," Rockwell said.

In July, members of the crew scattered to hook up with other projects or start graduate school. They may or may not be back the following year, which means Rockwell is always looking for crew.

Because Rockwell's work is supported by the Smithsonian Institution, her crew cruises around northern Michigan in two vehicles with U.S. government license plates. Brounce says he's amused by the reaction of the locals when shaggy-looking kids climb out of the government cars. He's also getting used to the suspicious looks that often come his way from local sheriff's deputies.

Their fieldwork starts around dawn most mornings from May through July. That means the early spring work is often done with frost coating the trees and a bite in the air. By late May there is a different bite in the air—swarms of blackflies that Falatek refers to as her "entourage." On this mid-June morning, however, a weak sun has trouble piercing a thick fog and the temperature hovers in the upper thirties. Ravens call in the distance and brown thrashers sing nearby as Rockwell, Brounce, and Demko carry armfuls of gear through a jack pine plantation to get to the territory of an unbanded male. It's an ankle-twisting, knee-wrenching, pants-drenching, face-scratching, disorienting hike. Along the way, Rockwell explains that the team is making a last-ditch attempt to capture males that have either eluded them or arrived late and just recently defined a nesting territory, and this is the second attempt to catch this particular male. Most males arrive in May and have already been captured.

Besides taking the tissue samples, the team plans to give this male a unique set of bands that will identify him to researchers both here and in the Bahamas. After Rockwell unfurls the netting, Demko sets up a pair of speakers and turns on a recording of a male Kirtland's warbler song. Although the birds tolerate the human intrusion fairly well, a male Kirtland's warbler will often aggressively confront another male who dares to enter his territory. Within a minute of hearing the recording, this male flies to the top of a nearby northern pin oak tree to check things out. Not actually seeing another male, he flies directly over the mist net and disappears. Rockwell is puzzled. "Usually the unbanded ones are pretty naïve and usually smack right in there," she says. However her experience also tells her that the late-arriving birds tend to be less dominant and are therefore less likely to attack an intruder.

It's a disappointment, but not a total failure; this male has a mate, and there is still a nest that needs to be checked. Rockwell and the others are careful around the nests. Since they will check each active nest three times during the nesting season they try to approach from a different direction each time they visit to keep a predator from catching on to the nest's location. They also wear tall rubber boots to cut down on any scent trail.

The nest is well hidden on the ground near the base of a jack pine tree and is essentially a cave of thick grasses. As Rockwell approaches within two feet, the female flushes, flies to a low branch just a couple feet away, and halfheartedly fakes a broken wing in an attempt to lure Rockwell away. As the female flutters, Rockwell peers into the nest and smiles; there are four tiny pink eggs inside. She quickly retreats to put her data on a form: date and time, stage of nest, number of adults attending, number of eggs and/or number of young. She adds one more critical piece of information: specific directions on how to find the nest in case one of her colleagues is the next to visit.

Unable to capture the male, Rockwell leaves Demko and Brounce to their fieldwork, gets in a car, and heads off to join Falatek and Banfield. The drive takes Rockwell out of this outwash plain, over a glacial moraine dominated by tall, lush hardwoods, and back down into another outwash plain. The moraines are only about thirty feet higher than the plains, but the difference in the vegetation is astounding.

The rest of the day would be like Rockwell's first stop of the morning: a mixed success. An attempt to capture a different unbanded male is unsuccessful, so the three turn their attention to checking the progress of nests they know about and finding new ones. Under what is

Sarah Rockwell sets up a mist net on a chilly, foggy June morning in hopes of catching a male Kirtland's warbler. If she catches the bird, she will band it and follow it as part of her study.

now a clear sky and blazing sun, Rockwell, Banfield, and Falatek strip off a couple of layers and pause to sort through data cards. They set their courses, consult their handheld Global Position System (GPS) units, and head out in different directions. At her first two stops, Rockwell finds the nests quickly, takes a peek, records her data, and moves on. She is able to find the nests quickly because pink vinyl tape hangs from branches in a rough triangle around the nest. Directions written on one piece of tape—"Nest is b/w 2 flags on the east side of ditch directly adjacent to the cluster of 2 J-pines. Hole faces east"—take Rockwell right to the nest. The next stop, however, is going to be more difficult. It's a spot on the map marked as the territory of a banded male known as WRRA. He was given that name for the combination of bands he wears on his legs: white over red on the left, red over aluminum on the right. Here Rockwell's challenge is to find the nest.

Using GPS, Rockwell navigates through the pines and quickly finds WRRA singing on a branch of a northern pin oak. The chase is on! Based on experience, Rockwell knows that the male will *eventually* lead her to the nest, but it will take tremendous patience. A Kirtland's warbler's territory can be as large as thirty acres, and the male may visit the nest only about once an hour to bring food to his mate while she is incubating. Furthermore, the male doesn't really want to give away the nest's location. So, if Rockwell approaches too closely, the male will make a wide circle around the nest without going to it. Or he may even drop the food he's carrying and leave the area.

For fifteen minutes, Rockwell follows the male in a fifty-yard semi-circle around a one-acre, football-shaped opening. Eventually the male leads Rockwell back to the pin oak where she first found him, only now she is on the opposite side of the tree. Just when Rockwell is about to kick a stump out of frustration, the female appears out of nowhere, low in the pin oak.

Rockwell retreats to the jack pines and hunkers down, her heart racing. Within a few seconds the female dives down into the blueberries and sweet ferns. Jackpot! Rockwell gets out her data cards and a roll of pink tape. She cuts three ribbons, each about eighteen inches long, and marks two with "18R," which means that this is Rockwell's eighteenth nest of the year. Keeping with protocol, she writes a description of how to find the nest on the third ribbon. She also admits that she's glad she found this nest because there is a friendly rivalry among the researchers to see who can find the most nests—and she is barely ahead of Brounce.

Sharpie marker and ribbons stuffed in a pocket, Rockwell heads for the nest. After a few minutes of searching she finds it, peeks inside, records her data, and retreats to start the process of finding the next nest.

Research like Rockwell's has opened up a new world of knowledge about the Kirtland's warbler, but much of that information would be worthless without one critical bit of knowledge: how many Kirtland's warblers are there? If wildlife biologists are going to manage for them, knowing where they are and how many there are is pretty important.

Held annually since 1971, the Kirtland's warbler census is viewed as an important gauge of the species' health, but in its own way it has also become an annual event. In early June, people come from all over Michigan to count Kirtland's with either the Michigan Department of Natural Resources or the U.S. Forest Service. On this morning, counters for the DNR start gathering at 6:30 a.m. at the intersection of two unmarked dirt roads in northwestern Ogemaw County. They drink coffee from gigantic plastic mugs and rock back and forth trying to stay warm. It doesn't matter if people mill around in the middle of the intersection; there's no traffic, nor will there be for a while. Although the sky is overcast, there are broken clouds and the sun occasionally breaks through. The rain that fell overnight has moved out, but nearly everyone is still dressed head to toe in waterproof clothing and boots. The clothing has a secondary benefit—it helps to fend off the numerous mosquitoes. Things will only get worse for the census takers once they head into the jack pines; there the mosquitoes will be replaced by blackflies.

Rockwell and her team are here, as are Jerry Weinrich, Elaine Carlson, Mike Petrucha, and several other employees and retirees of the Michigan DNR. Carol Bocetti, a professor of biology at California University in Pennsylvania and leader of the Kirtland's Warbler Recovery Team, has made the trip, along with her two preteen children, her sister, and her sister's two teenage girls. It's a good turnout this morning: twenty-three people. While the census leaders decide which participants will be taking which census areas, one DNR employee uses his boot to scratch out a line in the sand road. Then he measures the length of one chain—sixty-six feet—and draws another line in the sand. Immediately, people begin to count how many paces it takes to walk between the two lines. Some do it two or three times. It's critically important that they get it right because it's the way they will measure the distance they walk between stops to listen for singing male Kirtland's. It's not critical to stop every sixty-six feet if no birds are singing or if those that are singing are still quite a distance ahead, but it is important to know how many chains one has completed so the data will be accurate. After a quick meeting to pass out maps and compasses, assign locations, and explain protocol, the group breaks up and heads off in different directions.

Mike Petrucha looks at his map and sighs. He's been assigned a transect that will take him through some of the thickest jack pines. It can't be as bad as his first year on the survey, however. That year, while two of Petrucha's friends were assigned to nearby transects that went through the jack pine, he got one that went right down the middle of a road. At the end of the day, when people were comparing notes, the chief of the survey team lamented that he had finished his transect nearly a quarter mile from where he was supposed to come out. Instead of leaving well enough alone, Petrucha cracked that he had walked his transect exactly the way he needed to and came out exactly where he was supposed to. The next day Petrucha was assigned to a transect with a beaver pond in the middle of it. Today he would learn the hard way that his transect had a bog in the middle of it, and he would emerge from the jack pine midmorning with his shoes full of water and his pant legs wet up to his knees.

A beaver pond might not be the worst thing that a census worker encounters. That's because they annually check nesting habitat on a former U.S. Air Force target range that is now the Pine River Kirtland's Warbler Management Area and Michigan National Guard's Camp Grayling. Both sites are known to contain unexploded artillery shells and ammunition. The Pine River site is only about two hundred acres, and the Department of Defense has told the U.S. Forest Service that it should stop activities in the area until the bombs are cleared.

According to Paul Thompson, the U.S. Forest Service wildlife biologist responsible for the area, the bombs were discovered after the area was clear-cut and a bulldozer hauling a giant roller chopper had gone through the area to cut up the slash to help it break down faster. More bombs were unearthed when yet another bulldozer using a V-shaped plow to cut a furrow into the ground started working its way through the area in preparation for planting trees. Plowing was stopped immediately when the bulldozer started dislodging bombs that had been embedded in the ground.

Thompson says that even though technically these are bombs, they are not as dangerous as *real* bombs because instead of being filled with explosives, they are filled with sand or phosphorus. Only the tips of the bombs contain a small amount of black power, which would detonate on impact and release the inert center. The sand or phosphorus "explosion" allows training officers to judge how accurate the pilots had been without destroying the training target. But the bombs are still dangerous because black powder becomes more unstable with age, and even though none of them exploded when they were dug up by the plow the last time through, there's no guarantee that they won't explode on contact in the future.

Thompson says the Forest Service still conducts a census in this area every year, but volunteers are given much more training before entering the area, and Forest Service employees guide the volunteers through the most dangerous areas.

Although Weinrich has never seen unexploded bombs at Pine River, he has seen them on Camp Grayling land, including some with the marks of porcupine teeth on them.

He has found the experience of doing a Kirtland's warbler census on Camp Grayling to be no big deal.

"You just have to watch where you walk," he laughs.

Weinrich starts his Ford Ranger pickup truck and heads out. In this, his thirty-seventh census, he has been assigned an easy route. Rather than walking through the jack pine forest, he gets to walk a road. Asked how he drew such an easy assignment, he has a quick answer: "I'm old!"

Weinrich is a bridge that spans two eras—from Walkinshaw and Mayfield to the current generation of biologists and foresters. Besides Bill Irvine, it's unlikely that anyone else alive has done as much for the warbler as Weinrich. His aura is enhanced by his smoky baritone voice, which gives him an immediate air of authority. Although Weinrich is from Michigan, he spurned a state school in favor of Iowa State University for his master's degree, because there he was given a chance to travel to the Antarctic to study penguins. He eventually retired from the DNR after spending thirty-one years in various positions,

Jerry Weinrich, a retired Michigan Department of Natural Resources wildlife biologist, counts singing birds during the annual Kirtland's warbler census in Ogemaw County, Michigan.

including as an endangered species biologist in the Roscommon, Michigan, field office. After all these years, you might think that Weinrich would be bored or fed up with searching for warblers. Not so. "I still want to be involved. It's still fun," he says.

Especially today. Weinrich likes the weather conditions. Despite the clouds and overcast, it's not too hot or cold and the wind is light. "As long as the wind doesn't pick up, yeah, this is good," he says.

The wind makes it harder to hear the birds and judge distances. Furthermore, it will cause the birds to sing from lower in the trees as they hunker down, so their songs won't carry as far. Unlike the others, who were dressed for tromping through a wet forest, Weinrich is dressed in an orange fleece jacket over a khaki shirt with a pack of cigarettes in the breast pocket. Conspicuously absent are binoculars. He says he doesn't need them when he's *listening* for birds. He's also wearing baggy corduroy pants and a pair of casual shoes. It's not what you would expect a professional field biologist to look like.

Weinrich reaches his starting point, parks his truck on the shoulder of the road, gets out, and starts listening. An upland sandpiper makes a spooky, rolling call from nearby. Brewer's blackbirds call from a nearby stand of knee-high jack pine saplings. Weinrich can also hear Kirtland's singing, but he won't count a bird he hears until he's sure he has walked beyond it. That way he can differentiate between the birds he has counted and the ones he has yet to count. He walks sixty-six feet, stops, listens, and points in the direction of each Kirtland's he hears singing.

"There's a bunch of birds here," he murmurs with a smile. With a pencil in his right hand and a clipboard in his left propped against his torso, he stands erect and points in the direction of each Kirtland's he hears singing. When one Kirtland's sings, two or three other males will often respond. Each male Kirtland's will sing as a way of signaling their territory, and other males in the area will sing back as a way of saying, "I'm over here, and this is my territory." Weinrich listens carefully to a male with an unusually short song. He suspects that this bird has changed its song because he's at the edge of its territory and is uncertain of himself. Weinrich says that once this male gets back to the middle of his territory, he'll likely return to his full song.

Weinrich has to focus his hearing to isolate each warbler's song and differentiate it from those of the other birds in the area—hermit thrushes, chipping sparrows, field sparrows, and Nashville warblers. Singing brown thrashers pose a particular problem because they can imitate the calls of other birds, including the Kirtland's warbler. Weinrich takes his time—perhaps more than is really necessary—to make certain his count is correct.

Weinrich is among the most experienced participants on the census—and this is a time when experience counts. Skepticism about some of the totals has been increasing, as some numbers from some areas seem unusually large. Elaine Carlson, a wildlife biologist with the Michigan DNR and one of the key coordinators of the census, says the issue comes down to the experience of the volunteer. She believes that a few of the volunteers are confusing other birds' songs with that of the Kirtland's warbler or they are double counting by counting singing birds both ahead of and behind them.

This is a good day. Weinrich counts several birds but won't have a final number until he can compare his numbers and locations with those of other census takers who have walked parallel routes through the jack pine. If they all walked parallel courses and accurately kept track of their stopping points, it should be easy to determine where the birds were singing, plot their locations on a map, and get an accurate total for this tract. It's a long way from the bad old days of the 1970s and 1980s when Weinrich and other counters could spend days in the jack pines without seeing or hearing a single Kirtland's warbler. Weinrich remembers those days all too well, as record low populations led the recovery team to consider radical action. The first idea the team discussed was a cross-fostering plan that would have humans remove Kirtland's warbler eggs from their nests and place them in the nests of other warbler species to be raised by surrogate parents. A similar cross-fostering program in the early 1980s put whooping crane eggs in the nests of sandhill cranes in Idaho. That plan successfully restored the breeding whooping crane population west of the Rockies. Ultimately a cross-fostering plan was rejected for the warbler because biologists identified several problems.

> There hadn't been any previous attempts to cross-foster passerines. Since the concept was unproven, the Kirtland's Warbler Recovery Team was unwilling to take a risk that could ultimately damage the population even more.
>
> There was concern that the young Kirtland's warbler would imprint on the foster parents, causing the young bird to believe it was something other than a Kirtland's. Researchers have documented cases of young birds developing abnormal songs after being subjected to the songs of other bird species, and in the worst-case scenario, a Kirtland's warbler might even attempt to breed with members of the surrogate species.

Carol Bocetti, leader of the Kirtland's Warbler Recovery Team and a professor of biology at California University of Pennsylvania, counts birds with her children Tony and Julie during the annual Kirtland's warbler census.

> Once eggs had been removed from a Kirtland's nest, it would be very difficult to protect them from predators; even one egg lost from such a small population would represent a major setback.

One of the worst ideas for monitoring Kirtland's warblers bubbled up from a researcher with the U.S. Geological Survey who wanted to track the movements of young birds between the time they left the nest and the time they started migrating. Although the researcher's team had already received a permit from the DNR to work with Kirtland's warblers, it was quickly rescinded when details of the project surfaced. The researcher planned to attach radio transmitters to hatch-year Kirtland's warblers using elastic from underwear.

In 1986, Carol Bocetti, an Ohio State University master's degree student, would propose a radical idea that the warbler team thought worth exploring based on direction from the Fish and Wildlife Service's 1985 Kirtland's Warbler Recovery Plan: in the event that the population fell to a critically low level, Kirtland's warblers should be trapped and placed in captivity for the winter. The plan Bocetti proposed would have the warblers captured in the late summer in northern Michigan and relocated to the Columbus Zoo in Ohio, where they would spend the winter in the safety of an aviary. The following spring the birds would be transported to northern Michigan and released in young jack pine habitat in hopes that these birds would establish a new colony and subsequently use this habitat for several years to come. One of the benefits of this plan would be to prevent much of the mortality that occurs during migration.

To prepare for a winter captivity program, Bocetti would need to build a new aviary. She asked engineers at Owens-Corning to determine which type of insulation would best control outside noise and quizzed bird curators at the National and the Minneapolis Zoos for input on the aviary's design. The aviary was built in the basement of the Herbivore/Carnivore Building and consisted of eighteen separate cages, or "modules," built around a central work room/kitchen and a medical room. Each module was four feet wide, ten feet long and eight feet high. Each contained twelve artificial pine branches, a roosting platform located high in each corner, and a three-foot-tall artificial pine tree. The floor was covered with wood chips, and one wall was covered with a soft, feltlike material that would give the birds something to cling to. The lighting system was programmed to the Florida winter light cycle, automatically turning on at 6:00 a.m. and turning off at 6:00 p.m.

Before condemning a Kirtland's warbler to a winter's purgatory in central Ohio, Bocetti would test her procedures and the aviary on Nashville warblers, a much more common and widespread species that shares the Kirtland's warbler's northern Michigan habitat. In the late summer of 1986, Bocetti caught and banded forty juvenile Nashville warblers. Before transferring the birds to Columbus, they were held in aviaries on the sites where they would be released the following spring. Bocetti hoped that if the birds were introduced to this area premigration they would stay on the site and reproduce when they were released.

Bocetti's work resulted in an article that appeared in the winter 1995 issue of the *Wildlife Society Bulletin* on how to design aviaries and procedures to reduce mortality of captive warblers.

Bocetti's work on Nashville warblers led directly to her first field-work with Kirtland's warblers, which she conducted for her doctoral dissertation, also from Ohio State. "Density, Demography, and Mating Success of Kirtland's Warblers in Managed and Natural Habitats" asked whether Kirtland's warblers displayed a preference for a jack pine forest that had naturally regenerated after a fire over a jack pine plantation where trees were planted by machines. Bocetti found that female Kirtland's warblers clearly preferred the wildfire habitat to the plantations. After she compared the ground cover in the two areas, the reason for the preference became obvious: the warbler preferred the height of the lowest live branches and the size of the openings in the postfire vegetation.

As a result of her work, Bocetti recommended that plantations have smaller but more frequent openings to increase the length of the forest edge. She also urged forest managers not to kill oak and cherry stumps by spraying them with herbicide after clearing the land for planting. Both of Bocetti's recommendations were incorporated in the management plan and have proven to be helpful to the birds.

Bocetti has spent most of her adult life working with endangered species but never considered herself a bird person until she became involved with the Kirtland's warbler. "When I was an undergraduate," she said, "I did not think it would be a little dinky bird that caught my attention. I was into large carnivores. I did work on the Florida panther, and I was interested in black bears." But when it came time to interview for a graduate project, Bocetti found that the warbler project had all the elements she was looking for. "It was an easy choice for me. Once I got involved, I was sold on it. And never went away."

In the twenty years in which Bocetti has been involved with various endangered species, no other animal has captured her imagination like the Kirtland's. "First of all," she said, "the species is an amazing species. They let you into their lives, so it's easy to get attached right away. . . . I mean intimately in terms of being in the woods, being on the territory, watching the mating, watching the feeding of the babies, raising their

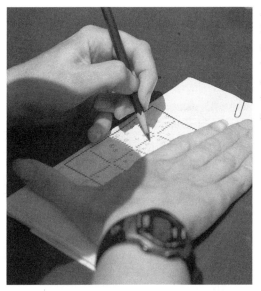

After walking her transect, Bocetti compares the locations of singing male Kirtland's warblers with the observations of other census takers who walked nearby transects to avoid overcounting the birds.

families. I mean, seriously, letting me into their family rearing—their lives. It's pretty awesome!" During the time Bocetti has spent with the warbler, she has learned that there is only one day when the adult Kirtland's do not want her or any other human around—the day the young leave their nests for the first time. On that day, she has noticed that the adults are unusually nervous, and their agitated behavior and scolding calls show that they are uncomfortable with a human around. When she encounters that situation, she does her best to respect the warbler's wishes and leaves.

While Bocetti was in the field collecting data for her two degrees, she was also collecting something else: Kirtland's warbler droppings. From 1986 to 1992, Bocetti and those who worked with her collected hundreds of fecal samples from the eight hundred birds they banded. The samples were scooped up from a tarp laid on the ground underneath a mist net or from the inside of the cotton bags the birds were put in for temporary holding. Each sample was then placed in a small glass vial and preserved in a 10 percent formalin solution. A small percentage of the vials were sent to a lab to be tested for disease, while the

rest were stored away in hopes that the right person would come along and examine each sample for clues to the warbler's diet.

The right person arrived at Michigan State University in the late 1990s in the form of Christie Deloria-Sheffield. Deloria-Sheffield was a recent graduate of Lake Superior State University and had been hired by the U.S. Fish and Wildlife Service to run the cowbird-trapping program. She had experience working with the piping plover along Lake Superior but had never even seen a Kirtland's warbler. Shortly after she started working for the Fish and Wildlife Service she realized that as a temporary hire she had a good chance to get a permanent job with the agency if she got a master's degree. With Michigan State's campus just a few miles from her office, it was an opportunity she could not pass up. Shortly after enrolling, she met with her adviser and Bocetti. It was then that she agreed to do the fecal analysis as her thesis. She was soon presented with hundreds of vials of liquefied warbler poop.

"It wasn't the sexiest project," Deloria-Sheffield said. "Just imagine you're a twenty-something-year-old person and you want to get your master's degree, and you get handed all these teensy-tiny vials of bird poop."

Instead of getting discouraged, Deloria-Sheffield dove in, so to speak. She quickly discovered that it was easy to separate the undigested bits of insects or seeds from the rest of the matter. She could just pick a bit out of the liquid, place it on a slide and examine it under a microscope. Identifying an undigested seed was easy. Identifying bits of legs, wings, mouthparts, and exoskeletons was a bit more problematic. Deloria-Sheffield compared what she saw through the microscope to illustrations in books or to a reference collection of insects and spiders that she had collected in the warbler's jack pine habitat. She also got help from an entomologist in Georgia who gave her clues about what to look for and helped her understand what she was seeing.

"With some things, I just couldn't tell what they were," Deloria-Sheffield said. "If I found the head of an ant, I could say, 'Okay, this black exoskeleton is an ant.' Wings come through whole. So do spider parts. Those were pretty distinctive."

Did it ever gross her out to think that she was looking at insects that had just come through the digestive tract of a bird? "Um, no, not

Kirtland's warbler nesting areas in northern lower Michigan are well posted. During nesting season entry is allowed only for researchers with a permit and people participating in the annual census. To keep disturbance to a minimum, the census takes place in early June, before the birds start to nest.

really," Deloria-Sheffield said. "Does that say something about me? I guess if I was picking through coyote or fox [feces], maybe there would have been a little bit more of the gross-out factor. It was a vial with liquid with stuff in it. If you're a fisheries and wildlife person it's no big deal. We're just sort of different."

With the pending return of the warblers to northern Michigan in the first week of May, Deloria-Sheffield had to temporarily abandon her research to attend to the cowbird-trapping program and another duty that came with the job: leading bird-watchers on the Kirtland's warblers tours out of Grayling. She recalls that it seemed odd to ask someone who had never seen a Kirtland's warbler to lead a tour of people eager to see the bird. What made the situation worse is that it took a while for the warblers to show up that May, and she had to take several tour groups into the field before she herself saw her first warbler. She also admits that she never revealed her secret.

"I had never seen it before, yet I was leading the tour. I was the expert," Deloria-Sheffield said with a laugh. "It probably was not the ideal situation."

Deloria-Sheffield's work seems minor compared to the contributions of Norman Wood, Nathan Leopold, Josselyn Van Tyne, Harold Mayfield, and Lawrence Walkinshaw. But her work, combined with that of the others, has helped to answer nearly every question critical to understanding the Kirtland's warblers' needs on their nesting grounds. Wildlife biologists now know what the Kirtland's warbler eats, how it nests, how much area it needs, and the best way to manage the forests for it.

But at the end of the summer, when the warbler leaves the jack pines, it flies off into uncertainty.

NINE : Scientists, Entrepreneurs, Dealmakers, Diplomats

Puzzled by the decline of Kirtland's Warbler on its nesting ground
where it is well-known, we are prompted to wonder about its survival
problems on the wintering ground where it is virtually unknown. It spends
more than half of each year in the Bahama Islands, but it is hard to find
there. Although it has been reported at some time on nearly all the larger
islands, it has been found nowhere regularly, and we have no inkling
of any special winter habitat niche.

—*Harold Mayfield*

It's early August in Mio, and the first signs of autumn are starting to
appear. The sun is lower in the sky, casting noticeably longer shad-
ows than a month earlier. The days can still be blisteringly hot, but the
nights are longer and refreshingly cooler. With kids on vacation from
school, families in canoes and inner tubes head down the Au Sable
River for a day of fun. They seem to be taking their time as they drift
down the river, but really they are rushing to cram in as much as they
can before Labor Day and the start of school. Trucks hauling huge
tree trunks rumble their way through town several times a day, turning west onto M-72, heading for the mill in Grayling. There's a sense
of urgency to get as much timber in as possible before the weather
changes and logging roads turn into impassable bogs.

There are signs of change in the jack pine, too. Many of the plants
and grasses that provided cover for the Kirtland's warbler nests are
now brown and dry, and there's a hint of color in the hardwoods in
the distance.

The shorter days that come with the approaching equinox trigger physiological changes in the Kirtland's warbler and other migrants. It's a change that sets off a sense of urgency. It's time to go.

Although the young Kirtland's warblers have been out of the nest only a couple of months or so, they have already left home. The focus now is on the coming migration. But before a Kirtland's can leave the jack pines it must undergo a molt and replace all its feathers. A molt is a slow process that uses a tremendous amount of the bird's energy as worn feathers are sequentially replaced with fresh ones. Then it must prepare itself for an even bigger danger: migration. With each passing day, the risk of frost increases. The once abundant caterpillars that came with the first big insect hatch in the spring are gone. So are most of the blueberries, which provide water, carbohydrates, and lipids. Luckily there are other things to eat. Spiders and most insects provide protein and carbohydrates, while an aphid—little more than sugar and water—is the equivalent of a cup of Kool-Aid. The bird rushes to gorge itself on whatever it can find. It's time to go.

It's a quiet mid-August afternoon, but this Kirtland's warbler can sense a change coming; a cold front is approaching. As the afternoon shifts to evening, the wind picks up and the warbler and thousands of other birds rise out of the forests and into the early evening sky. Although they are all heading out together, they are not departing in any organized manner; it's every bird for itself. An overcast sky keeps the warbler from being able to see the stars, but it instinctively knows which way to go.

It is now dark as the warbler approaches Detroit. The lights of the tall buildings downtown draw its attention, and the bird heads straight for a window on the thirtieth floor of an office building. At the last second, a wind gust knocks the warbler from its path, and the bird passes just inches from the building, traveling nearly sixty miles an hour.[1]

Unlike spring migration, where the goal is to get to the jack pine as quickly as possible to be able to compete for the best territory and most desirable mate, the warbler travels at a more leisurely pace in the fall. If the weather is good and the food and cover plentiful, it might linger for a couple of days. But even with excellent conditions, the sense of urgency takes over. Again, it's time to go.

The Kirtland's warbler is luckier than some migrants because most of its journey is over land. A blackpoll warbler, on the other hand, may jump off the southern coast of New England and fly nonstop over the Atlantic Ocean to the West Indies or Brazil. A Kirtland's warbler, fortunately, can stop several times to rest and refuel, but the decision about where to stop is critical. A warbler leaving the jack pine will find significantly different ecosystems and habitats along the way. It can encounter wooded pockets on the southern coast of Lake Erie, monocultures in the farmlands of central Ohio, the mixed forests of the Appalachian Mountains, the pine-oak woodlands in the piedmont of the southern Atlantic coast, the pine forests of the Deep South, or the scrub of Florida.

And the warbler doesn't know what kind of conditions it will encounter along the way. In the worst-case scenario, a tropical weather system may force this warbler to land someplace with little food and no cover. If the warbler is forced down in a location with little food, the fat put on in an earlier stop will sustain it for a day or two. Or the bird may land in an excellent spot with lots of food and cover but one that is already occupied by several other birds. That may sound like an ideal situation, but it might not be. The more birds are concentrated in one area, the less food there will be for any individual.

Before long, the warbler has reached the Atlantic coast. From there, the next stop is one of the islands in the Bahamas, which may be hundreds of miles away. This warbler, however, has lost so much fat in coming this far that it no longer has enough to ensure safe passage. If the warbler leaves now, it would be taking a tremendous chance. Nevertheless, the restlessness of migration takes over and the warbler takes off with a fresh northwesterly wind. The risky decision soon turns into a crisis. Halfway across the Gulf Stream, with no land in sight, the wind shifts. The bird is now heading into the wind. With no place to stop, the only choice is to push on. With its fat reserves gone, the warbler begins to metabolize its muscles for energy, essentially cannibalizing itself. For more energy, the warbler will undergo another anatomical change; it will metabolize its internal organs, and its digestive system will atrophy. The situation is now critical.

There! Up ahead! In the predawn glow, the warbler can see a pine-covered island on the horizon. Once over the beach, the exhausted warbler drops from the sky and tumbles into the dune plants, breathing heavily. There's a spider on the underside of a leaf, which the warbler snatches and gobbles down. The journey is nearly over. The Kirtland's warbler has reached the Bahamas.

Even though there's no sign on the beach that reads "Welcome to the Bahamas," Dr. Joe Wunderle, Dr. David Ewert, and the other members of the Kirtland's Warbler Research and Training Project team have put out the welcome mat. Wunderle, a research wildlife biologist with the U.S. Forest Service's International Institute of Tropical Forestry (IITF) in Puerto Rico, and Ewert, a senior conservation scientist with the Nature Conservancy's field office in Lansing, Michigan, have gathered a team of workers on the island of Eleuthera to learn the answers to the last critical questions about the Kirtland's warbler. What is its preferred winter habitat? What can be done to ensure the habitat is preserved? Why does it choose a certain spot? What does it eat?

Unlike the thousands of snowbirds and tourists who flock to the Bahamas every winter to escape the cold, the Kirtland's warbler comes for the food. While the tourists spend the winter lounging on beautiful beaches and admiring the pristine blue water, the Kirtland's warblers quietly spend their time in the dense vegetation.

Take a closer look at that vegetation and it's easy to understand why the Kirtland's warbler is attracted to Eleuthera. Even though these are broadleaf plants, early succession coppice is similar to jack pine in that it grows in uneven patches and is dense near the ground. Unlike northern Michigan, the vegetation here mostly grows on rocky limestone. But like the jack pine region, there's a regular cycle of disturbance that keeps the vegetation from growing too tall or old to support the warblers' needs.

Wunderle's round glasses and salt-and-pepper beard give him the countenance of a college professor. He joined the IITF at a time when Puerto Rico was recovering from being deforested for agriculture in the 1930s and 1940s. The institute's mission was to reforest the island

Joseph Wunderle, a research wildlife biologist with the U.S. Forest
Service's International Institute of Tropical Forestry in Puerto Rico,
examines a wilted snowberry plant. The berries are an important part of
the Kirtland's warbler's winter diet in the Bahamas.

and develop a wood products industry. Since joining the IITF, he has
spent much of his time conducting research on birds in the West Indies
and Central America.

The IITF's wildlife program started in the 1970s with an effort to
conserve the Puerto Rican parrot, which is far closer to extinction
than the Kirtland's warbler. While the Kirtland's low point was fewer
than four hundred birds in 1974 and again in 1987, the population of
the Puerto Rican parrot was as low as thirteen birds in 1973. The parrot population recovered somewhat in the 1980s, but it took a hit from
Hurricane Hugo in 1989. The species entered the twenty-first century
with a population of fewer than forty birds.

Wunderle got involved in migratory bird research on Puerto
Rico when his colleagues documented a major decline in the number of migrants in their winter bird population monitoring project on
the south coast of the island. That study is now the longest-running

research project in the tropics. He's also been conducting migrant studies across the Caribbean since the 1980s. Wunderle had virtually no experience with the Kirtland's warbler prior to forming the Kirtland's Warbler Research and Training Team. His only encounter with the species was briefly observing one while doing a survey for the warbler in the Turks and Caicos.

As one of the leaders of the Kirtland's Warbler Research and Training Project, he visits the island three times during the fieldwork season—in the fall when the warblers first arrive, in the middle of winter, and again in spring, just as the warblers are preparing to depart for the jack pine. When asked why he spends his winters in the tropics as opposed to the highly variable climate of his college days at the University of Minnesota and University of Maine, Wunderle dryly replied, "I prefer hurricanes."

Ewert, on the other hand, is tall, muscular, and clean shaven. He is a senior conservation scientist with the Nature Conservancy in Michigan, where he works on stopover sites for migratory birds in the Great Lakes region, protection of Great Lakes islands, and wind energy issues. While he may be less sterotypically professional in appearance, he is patient and every bit as willing to share his knowledge. Ewert has a doctorate in ornithology from the City University of New York in a joint program with the American Museum of Natural History and teaches ornithology at the University of Michigan's Biological Station near Pellston, Michigan, during the summer. Wunderle and Ewert have known each other since they were undergraduates and interns in an ornithology training program on Long Island, New York, in the late 1960s.

Ewert grew up in East Lansing, Michigan, and knew at an early age that he wanted to be an ornithologist. His first opportunity to do fieldwork on the Kirtland's warbler came in the mid-1980s, when he was asked to assess whether recording the Kirtland's song might be used as a method to accurately estimate the birds' numbers. Ewert was tapped for the job because his dissertation was on song variation in the eastern towhee. He spent two breeding seasons recording Kirtland's warbler songs and discovered that there simply wasn't enough variation in them to be able to accurately identify individuals by song alone.

David Ewert, a senior conservation scientist with the Nature Conservancy's Field Office in Lansing, Michigan, visits Eleuthera three times each winter to study the Kirtland's warbler's winter habitat.

As a result, the Michigan Department of Natural Resources and the U.S. Forest Service continued with the traditional method of counting birds by counting the songs of singing males by ear during the annual census.

Ewert visits Eleuthera twice during the field season, once in November and once in late March through early April. After the field-work is completed in the spring, he immediately jets back to Michigan to await the warblers' arrival in the jack pine. The two primary researchers may be on Eleuthera for only short periods during the winter, but they have a team of research assistants there to monitor the birds' every move from October 1 through the end of April.

The two researchers have taken part in dozens of studies, but on this particular one Wunderle and Ewert are more than just scientists, and their fieldwork is more than just another study. Working in an emerging country that lacks a strong conservation ethic requires that the two be diplomats and educators. And because they want to make sure that the Kirtland's warbler habitat is conserved for years to come, they are also advocates, dealmakers, brokers, and mentors.

The idea for a Kirtland's warbler field study in the Bahamas came out of a 1996 meeting Ewert and Wunderle had with leaders of the Bahamian government and the Bahamas National Trust at an ornithological conference. Even though Ewert and Wunderle had not yet built a partnership, they both suggested that Kirtland's warbler fieldwork in the Bahamas was critically important because so little was known about the bird's distribution and preferred habitat on its wintering grounds. The suggestion took a step closer to becoming reality in 1997 when the Nature Conservancy—with funding from Canon, the camera maker—brought four leaders of the Bahamas National Trust and the Ministry of Agriculture and Marine Resources to Michigan to meet members of the Kirtland's Warbler Recovery Team. That trip laid the groundwork for two years of negotiations that led the Americans and Bahamians to reach a consensus on three goals of any future research project.

a better understanding of the habitat

a better understanding of how Bahamian birds respond to drought during the Bahamian winter

a greater ability to conserve land and animals in the Bahamas by training Bahamian students as part of the Kirtland's Warbler Research and Training Project team and then providing funding for these students to attend undergraduate schools following completion of their work.

Even though Wunderle and Ewert were interested in understanding how all Bahamian birds use the scrub landscape, they knew they probably wouldn't get past passport control at the airport if they tried to enter the Bahamas to study only one species of particular interest in the United States. Wunderle has traveled throughout the Caribbean, and he and Ewert are sensitive to what it takes to get things done in the region. This often means that in order to conduct their research they need to help the host country accomplish something it wants done.

With a consensus on goals and objectives established, Wunderle, Ewert, and Eric Carey, the executive director of the Bahamas National Trust, wrote a proposal for funding the Bahamian work—and then the moon and the stars aligned. An administrator at the U.S. Forest Service's International Programs Office in Washington, DC, called Wunderle to say that the agency had received money to fund a winter field study on migrant birds with a focus on the Kirtland's warbler.

With the funding in place, Wunderle and Ewert started planning. Their first and most important task would not be something like making plane reservations or hiring a staff. The first task would be to lower expectations. Over the previous 130 years, some of the best ornithologists in the western hemisphere had thoroughly searched the Bahamas for the Kirtland's warbler with little or no success.

The historical prize for finding the most Kirtland's warblers goes to naturalist Charles Johnson Maynard of Newton, Massachusetts, who collected thirty-eight wintering Kirtland's warblers between 1884 and 1915, when the species' population would likely have been experiencing an unusual boom. Even with that incredible success, Maynard established the conventional wisdom about the wintering Kirtland's warbler, which he called a "shy bird of solitary habits."[2] The inability to find Kirtland's warblers during the winter over the next ninety years would only help to reinforce that idea.

In the 1930s, James Bond, an ornithologist with the Academy of Natural Sciences in Philadelphia and author of *Birds of the West Indies,* found only one Kirtland's warbler in one hundred days of searching.[3] Van Tyne and Mayfield spent fifty-nine man-days searching New Providence and Eleuthera for the Kirtland's warbler in 1949 and came up empty. John T. Emlen, the author of a monograph on Bahamas land birds, did not find a Kirtland's warbler during five hundred hours of surveying Grand Bahama and Andros islands between 1968 and 1971. Bruce E. Radabaugh spent eight hundred hours in the field during the winters and early springs of 1972 and 1973, surveying eleven islands, ranging from the pine islands of the northwest to the coppice islands of the southeast. For all his work, he found one Kirtland's warbler on the eastern end of Crooked Island.[4] Paul Sykes, a now retired research biologist with the U.S. Geological Survey, found three birds while searching the Bahamas and Turks and Caicos Islands in the mid-1980s. Sykes's work was cut short when the project's manager ran into problems that got the team kicked out of the Bahamas on three days' notice, effectively ending a three-year study just short of one full season.

Mayfield summed up everyone's frustrations in an article he wrote for the *Wilson Bulletin:* "Unless the birds are concentrated in some locality or in some unusual habitat not yet discovered, the prospect of finding them is discouraging indeed."[5]

Given the results of previous efforts, why should Wunderle and Ewert expect anything different?

Ewert and Wunderle established their field study on Andros, a pine-covered island between Nassau and Florida, in October 2001. They chose Andros because it was thought at the time that Kirtland's warblers could be found most often in pine-dominated habitats. The two researchers didn't really expect to find many Kirtland's warblers, so they set out to study how the bird community adapted to increasing drought through the winter. By studying other birds they hoped to extrapolate how a Kirtland's warbler might respond under the same conditions. Wunderle and Ewert chose this particular spot on Andros because it was being proposed for a new national park and their findings would contribute to management decisions.

In March 2002, Wunderle got an exciting call from Eric Carey. Carey told Wunderle to drop everything and get on the first flight to Eleuthera, because he and other members of the Ornithology Group of the Bahamas National Trust had just found eight Kirtland's warblers in coppice vegetation on Madeira Road in the southern part of Eleuthera.

Eight Kirtland's warblers in one spot? In coppice and not pines? Although Maynard wrote of finding multiple Kirtland's warblers in coppice in the late nineteenth century, no one had reported so many in one spot since.

Wunderle and two research assistants flew to Eleuthera as quickly as they could, and they quickly caught and color banded four Kirtland's warblers. A month later work and romance coexisted temporarily as Wunderle returned to the Madeira Road site with his wife to band two additional birds. After banding six Kirtland's warblers in one small area on Eleuthera and finding only a single bird on Andros, it was an easy decision at the conclusion of the field season to move the project.

With the start of the second research season in October 2002, a new group of research assistants and a new field director, David Currie, joined Wunderle and Ewert. Their efforts focused on the Madeira Road site until December 2002, when a dispute over ownership forced the team off the land. The loss of the Madeira Road site was a shock to the team, but it turned out to be a blessing in disguise.

It's 5:30 a.m. There's barely a glow in the eastern sky, but light floods out of a white concrete building on Lord Street in Tarpum Bay. While most residents of this tiny fishing village are still asleep, Wunderle, Ewert, and the other members of their team are not just awake but alert and ready to go. As the sun rises, they quietly pack their gear into the trunk of a beat-up gray Nissan and head out. The goal today is to be at the study site called Leary's Field early enough to open the nets at 6:30. It's only a fifteen-minute drive south on the Queen's Highway from their base in Tarpum Bay to the dead-end road that leads to the study site. Shortly after turning onto this unnamed road the pavement turns to dirt, the road narrows down to two tracks, and the vegetation closes in from the sides and above. About a mile up the road, there's a small opening on the left just large enough to serve as a shaded parking spot. It wouldn't matter if they parked in the middle of the road, however, because no one else will be driving through here. The team gathers backpacks filled with sunscreen and insect repellent, water jugs and granola bars, binoculars and banding gear, and heads farther up the road. It's a short walk around fallen trees and under a canopy of vines to a spot where they climb over a fence into an abandoned orchard. From there it's another short walk, past rows of overgrown fruit trees and crumbling PVC pipes, to the banding station. Although the station is the center of all the activities here, it's really nothing more than a portable card table under the shade of an old mango tree. The banding station was put here because its location wouldn't have an impact on the birds and nets and because it's the only clearing in the vegetation large enough to accommodate the team.

After dumping their gear, Ewert, Wunderle, and the research assis-

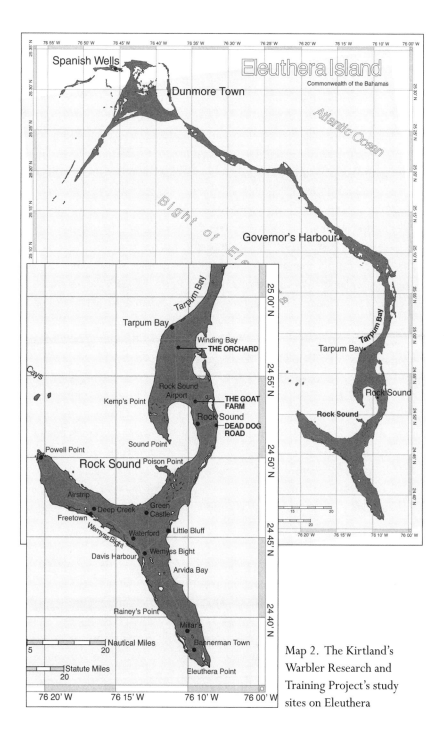

Map 2. The Kirtland's Warbler Research and Training Project's study sites on Eleuthera

tants head out to open four lines of mist nets. The team had worked in this area the previous evening and left the nets up but bundled closed, knowing they would be returning in just a few hours. Over the four years of the study, the team has never had a problem leaving nets in the bush. The fact that no one has ever disturbed them is a reflection of how life has changed on Eleuthera and across the Bahamas in general over the past few years. The children play in towns and rarely wander away from occupied areas. The old culture of deriving medicinal cures from native plants is gone, and the recipes are largely forgotten. No one goes into the bush anymore except to dump their unwanted furniture, automobiles, boats, toilets, fire trucks, television sets, bottles, and cans. Team members would prefer that this waste be properly disposed of, but they use the litter found on other sites to their advantage as landmarks to describe the locations where Kirtland's warblers have been found. This site, however, has almost no waste because of its remote location.

Leary's Field is owned by Robert Chappell, who also owns the nearby Rock Sound Club. That "club," built by Arthur Vining Davis, the industrialist and philanthropist, is now more a rejuvenated resort than an exclusive club for the wealthy. It's on the Queen's Highway about halfway between Tarpum Bay and Rock Sound. Chappell has happily allowed Ewert and Wunderle to use his land for their research, and in exchange the ornithologists are helping Chappell establish his resort as lodge for ecotourists. After four years in the bush, the two scientists know there are plenty of interesting birds on this part of the island, and they see potential for visiting birders to boost the area's sagging economy.

It's now after sunrise on Leary's Field. A bank of clouds just above the horizon hides the sun, but the orchard is alive with birdcalls. The only other sounds are the leaves quaking in a slight breeze and the footsteps of the team members on the rocky soil. Despite the good weather, the crew is pessimistic about the prospects for catching many birds today. They banded in this same area right up until sunset the previous day, and not only did they fail to capture any Kirtland's warblers, but they didn't see or hear any. As for other birds in the area, they should be on full alert. Wunderle says that once a bird has been caught it will remember the location of the net and avoid it.

Today's team consists of Wunderle; Ewert; Jen White, the project's field director who recently obtained her doctorate from the University of Missouri; Jen Thieme of Grand Rapids, Michigan; and Elise Corliss of Foxboro, Massachusetts. Scott Johnson, a student at the College of the Bahamas, is usually with the team, but today he is on a plane heading for Nassau to interview for his visa to attend school in the United States. The last member of the team is Alana Demko, who has the day off. Demko spent the previous summer in northern Michigan as part of Sarah Rockwell's crew and also spent the winter before that working with the Kirtland's warbler team here on Eleuthera. This year, however, is her Kirtland's swan song. She's off to Nevada at the end of this field season to join a team conducting research on the willow flycatcher.

After helping to open the nets, Thieme opens a plastic container that's large enough to fit a dozen or so cupcakes and starts laying out the tools needed for the day. There are multiple calipers, pliers, pens, a scale, a roll of adhesive tape, and a half dozen cotton swabs. And there are multiple containers of bands in various sizes so each bird can be given a properly sized band that won't fall off or be too tight.

For each first-time capture, workers record the species, age, gender, location, date, and time and carefully measure the length of wing, tail, tarsus (the foot), and beak. Other measurements, such as the amount of fat and the mass of the pectoralis muscle, are scored subjectively. Holding a bird on its back across the palm with the bird's neck held gently between the fore and middle fingers, a researcher separates the breast feathers by gently blowing on them or using a wet cotton swab to spread and mat them. Once the feathers are separated, it's easy to find and estimate the size of a pocket of yellow fat below the skin. The researchers also estimate the mass of the pectoralis muscle as an indicator of the bird's overall health. The bird is given a subjective score ranging from zero for no fat or a weak muscle to four for a butterball and a strong muscle. Banders measure its weight by sliding it headfirst into a toilet paper roll to immobilize it and then standing the roll up on a scale. Finally, the researchers extract the outermost right-hand tail feather. That feather will be analyzed for isotopes that will tell researchers where the bird came from. The feather often comes out with a little "pop." Wunderle admits it has to hurt a little bit, similar perhaps to having an individual hair pulled out of a human scalp. But he also knows the extraction does no permanent harm to the bird and the feather will grow back rapidly. The team captured one particular thick-billed vireo three times over the course of one field season. Every time the bird was caught one feather was extracted. Each time, by the time the bird was caught again three months later, the feather had fully grown in.

It doesn't take long before team members are plucking birds from the nets, sliding them into cotton bags and bringing them back to the banding station. The first capture this morning is a thick-billed vireo, a common bird on Eleuthera. This particular bird was caught at least once before and is already banded. Recaptured birds are valuable because they allow a fresh assessment of the bird's physical health, which reflects the overall condition of the habitat. As the amount and type of food change from fall to winter to spring, so will the health of the bird as measured by its weight and the amount of fat it carries. The data are collected in either of two journals: one for resident birds and one for migrants. The data on resident birds are especially valuable because so little is known about the population on Eleuthera, and this information will become a baseline for future studies.

It's a surprisingly productive morning. There is a regular stream of gray catbirds, bananaquits, American redstarts, ovenbirds, thick-billed vireos, and greater Antillean bullfinches. The banders treat each bird with care, but a bullfinch gets special treatment. While all the other birds get a lightweight aluminum band, the bullfinch gets a heavier steel band because it can crush an aluminum band with its large, powerful beak. The banders approach a bullfinch in the net with dread because if it has the strength to crush an aluminum band, imagine what it can do to a fingertip or the soft flesh on the back of a hand.

Being bitten by a bullfinch is painful, but there's another occupational hazard of bird banding: flying feces. While handling a catbird, Thieme's sky blue shirt is suddenly splattered with purple poop.

Jen White (left) and Jen Thieme (right) count fruit on a wild sage plant as part of a study on the availability of food consumed by the Kirtland's warbler during the winter months in the Bahamas.

Despite the disappointment and disgust of having a catbird ruin a clean shirt, Thieme keeps her focus and continues to work on the catbird until she finishes the job. After releasing the bird, Thieme inspects the damage on her shirt and finds a few berry seeds that have come through the bird's system undigested. She sweeps the seeds into a small brown paper envelope, which she labels and tucks away for later identification.

It's early April, and there are signs everywhere that a young bird's fancy is turning to love. Endemic Bahama mockingbirds are chasing each other in competition for the best nesting sites, and recently fledged bananaquits are showing up in the nets. The team takes extra care with these young birds, even taking them back to where they were caught to release them so they can be nearer to their parents.

This time of year, young male Kirtland's warblers prepare for the upcoming mating season by singing a "subsong," which is jumbled-up bits and pieces of the full nesting-ground song. This subsong, Wunderle says, is especially important for young males as they try to figure out what it takes to be all grown up. Unfortunately, not only have the researchers not heard any subsongs, but they haven't seen a Kirtland's warbler here in a couple days, so this will be their last visit for the remainder of this field season. It's clear to team members why the warblers have moved on: it has been several weeks since Eleuthera has seen rain, and the berries of the wild sage plants—an important food for the Kirtland's warbler—are dry and shriveled.

Winter is the dry season on Eleuthera and in the Bahamas in general. Cold fronts, originating in Canada, bring little more than occasional showers. March and April are the driest months of the year, which is bad for the birds that are preparing to migrate. Berries dry up. Insects become scarce. Depending on the severity of the drought, trees can lose their leaves and go dormant, and this year's drought is heading in that direction. The drought slowly abates as spring stretches into summer. Winds that had been from the west and northwest have shifted and now come from the east. Those moisture-laden winds off the warm Atlantic Ocean combine with hot sunshine to cause thunderstorms to develop over the islands. The heavy rain produced by those storms creates standing water, which helps the insect population explode. The abundance of rain also starts a new cycle of fruit production on the wild sage, black torch, and snowberry plants. By the time migrating birds return in late summer and early autumn, the islands are lush and food is plentiful.

Fall also brings the threat of hurricanes. Although there is no guarantee that Eleuthera will be struck in any given year, the island is hit often enough that there is a regular natural disturbance to the habitat. High winds blow down the tallest trees, and because the island is so flat, salt water from storm surges can kill vegetation for a considerable distance inland. Even though there is no evidence that any Kirtland's warblers have ever been killed by a hurricane, it's clear that a hurricane puts a tremendous amount of stress on any bird that gets caught in one. Not only does it take months for the vegetation to recover, but the hurricane also kills the fruit or drives off the insects these birds would use as food. Therefore, it's common for songbirds to leave a hurricane-damaged area until the vegetation and food recover, and that process may take years.

Winter rainfall can vary widely from year to year, often depending on sea temperature conditions thousands of miles away in the Pacific Ocean off the coast of Ecuador. In El Niño years, warm water pools in the Pacific, and the Bahamas tend to be wetter than normal. In La Niña years, cool water pools in the Pacific, and islands tend to be drier than normal. This year happens to be a La Niña year, and the drought is particularly severe.

The team can see the drought's impact in some of the birds they have netted because they have very little fat. That lack of fat may cause those that migrate to delay their departure or change their route. Concerned about the drought's impact on the Kirtland's warbler, the team will monitor the movements of their warblers much more closely now that migration is only a month away. They know from previous years that the warblers will move around the island to find food, and the best place to find food when there is a drought is another of the team's study sites, the Goat Farm.

Like Leary's Field, the Goat Farm is remote. Make a left-hand turn off the Queen's Highway near the airport in Rock Sound and drive up a dusty road to its end. Grab your gear and climb over a five-foot steel farm gate. From there, it's a half-mile walk across the limestone rubble and dusty soil and over a barbed-wire fence and gate to the study site.

It's already late afternoon before the team members arrive. They are not allowed onto the Goat Farm any earlier because the owner doesn't want his goats disturbed during the day. Researchers can use the area only after 3:30; the goats have been trained to come into the enclosure at that time every afternoon to avoid predators.

While the rest of southern Eleuthera is slowly drying up, the plants at the Goat Farm are lush and green. The water table is unusually high in this spot, and the berries that the Kirtland's warbler loves to eat are robust and plentiful.

"This is hog heaven for Kirtland's warblers," Ewert says.

Indeed, on the walk from the car to the study site, Ewert detects a Kirtland's warbler by its "chip" call. Within seconds, a male Kirtland's pops up to see who has strayed in to his territory. After studying this bird's habits and making notes, Ewert again heads for the study site. He's forced to pause a second time when another male Kirtland's pops up. Even though neither bird is banded, Ewert can tell these are different birds because their molt patterns give them distinctly different looks. In both cases, Ewert watches the birds carefully. He notes the date, time, location, gender, and whether the bird is banded. He then takes special notice of their foraging behavior. Both birds are gleaning insects rather than eating berries. Ewert estimates how far the insect was above the ground when the warbler found it and then estimates plant height from ground to top.

Ewert's observations of two different Kirtland's warblers eating insects are two more bits of data that should help answer the question of what the birds eat prior to migration—data that are currently at odds. Most of the team's personal observations indicate that a Kirtland's warbler will consume more fruit than insects. But, Wunderle says, stable isotopes in blood samples show that the birds eat more insects as the spring migration draws closer. He admits that the observational data may be skewed simply because it is easier to see a Kirtland's eating a berry on top of a plant than it is to see exactly what a bird is eating deep inside the thick vegetation. Although the Kirtland's warbler likes to eat the berries of black torch, snowberry, and wild sage, they lack protein. As a result, the warbler gets little more than sugar and water from them. But the very fact that the warbler tracks these berries demonstrates that they are important to the bird's diet.

Even though Ewert came to the Goat Farm to find Kirtland's warblers, it's clear these two birds heard his approach and came out to see him. The birds' actions seem to run counter to the conventional wisdom, developed over years of searching for Kirtland's warblers, which says these warblers are shy, quiet, and do their best to avoid human contact when they are on their winter grounds. Ewert says the behavior of these two birds doesn't necessarily contradict that notion because there is a lot of variation in the personalities of individual birds; some Kirtland's warblers are curious and aggressive, while others are more passive and cautious in the presence of humans. It's not a coincidence, however, that both of these birds are males. At both ends of their range, males are much more aggressive than females, with females making themselves highly conspicuous only when they are selecting mates on their arrival at the nesting grounds in May.

The team stumbled on the Goat Farm by accident when Dave Currie, the project's first field director, used radio telemetry to track a bird from the Madeira Road site to the farm. Currie received permission from the owner of the farm to enter the land and was immediately excited by what he saw. Wunderle says that when Currie returned from exploring the Goat Farm, he declared, "If there aren't other Kirtland's there, I'll eat my hat." Given how notoriously difficult it is to find Kirtland's warblers, Wunderle immediately started thinking in terms of serving hat salad, hat sandwiches, hat soup, and hat stew. Today the goat farm is a focus of Kirtland's research, and Currie's hat remains undigested. Wunderle gives Currie much of the credit for getting the Kirtland's warbler project established on Eleuthera by walking extensively across the southern part of the island looking for Kirtland's warblers and their habitat and talking with residents to build positive working relationships.

Currie joined the project in 2002, after coordinating research on two endangered bird species in the Seychelles in the Indian Ocean. Shortly after arriving on Eleuthera, however, he was forced to expand the search for Kirtland's warblers when a land dispute closed off the Madeira Road site. Currie, who describes himself as "intense" and a "pretty hard taskmaster," gathered satellite maps of southern Eleuthera to try to identify potential Kirtland's warbler habitat based on vegetation. Once an area had been deemed potentially suitable, team members would systematically search the area while playing a recording of a Kirtland's warbler song.

"Unfortunately you are unable to detect wintering Kirtland's warblers from a car," Currie says. "You have to have your nose pressed up close against the leaf litter to find them, and most of the time it is a thankless task."

Currie literally wore out boots searching for Kirtland's warblers—a pair for every year he was involved in the project. The value of those boots cannot be underestimated. In the first year alone, Currie and his assistants found more than twenty-five Kirtland's warblers and banded ten. And as a result of his efforts, the team established three new study sites—the Goat Farm, Dead Dog Road, and Rock Sound. They also found the first Kirtland's warbler in the Bahamas that had been banded in Michigan. More important, they shed important new light on the wintering habits of the Kirtland's warbler.

Besides wearing out boots, Currie recalls none too fondly a few other experiences in the Bahamian bush. There was the time he was chopping brush to establish a grid on a study site when he realized there was an odd weight on the left side of his head.

"There was only [one] thing that fit this feeling," Currie says. He bent over, quickly ran his gloved hand over his hair, and was not surprised to see a large tarantula plop at his feet. And there were the run-ins with poisonwood, a plant in the same family as poison sumac and cashew. The problem with poisonwood, Currie says, is you don't realize immediately that you have come in contact with the plant because it takes a couple days for a rash to develop. It took only one episode with poisonwood for Currie to learn how to avoid the plant.

And then there was the time Currie was clearing brush from a study site when he accidentally hit himself with a machete, gouging a deep gash in his leg and severing a vein. He was able to contact Wunderle via walkie-talkie and then crawl out of the bush, blood spurting from his leg. Wunderle helped Currie compress the blood flow at the wound site with a cloth and then drove him to the closest clinic with his bleeding leg elevated and sticking out of the car's window the length of the trip.

Currie left the project at the end of the 2006 field season to return to his partner and their son in Belgium. He says that when he left he had had enough. "Bahamian bush is thick—you do not walk through it by choice, and it is clear why the Kirtland's warbler winter ecology has remained an enigma for so long."

The discovery of so many Kirtland's warblers at the Goat Farm immediately got Ewert and Wunderle asking questions. What was special about this place that caused so many warblers to gather there? The answer was food. Why was there so much food there? The answer is that the goats act as a natural disturbance by eating the plants that compete with the warbler's preferred fruit plants, which allows the wild sage to prosper. So could the goat play a key role in Kirtland's warbler conservation in other parts of the Bahamas? The answer to that question could very well be yes, but to find out the ornithologists would need to persuade goat farmers to keep more goats. For goat farmers to take on more goats would require more access to more land for goat browsing so as to prevent overgrazing. That would mean extra expenses for the farmers, so Ewert and Wunderle would have to assure them that it is worth it. That has Wunderle and Ewert thinking about finding new markets for goat products—cheese, milk, and meat.

The idea is not that far-fetched. Goat meat is somewhat common in the Bahamian diet, and demand annually outstrips supply. The farmer who owns the land where this study is taking place says he could easily sell more goats for meat—if he only had more land for them to graze.

To find more land for more goats to graze, Wunderle has approached the electrical utility to see if managers would be willing to allow goats to graze under their power lines. The utility spends thousands of dollars every year to trim the vegetation under their lines, Wunderle argues, so think of how much money would be saved if goats were used for vegetation control rather than teams of humans. Wunderle and Ewert plan to gather additional information on goats' browsing habits before they draw up and institute a habitat management plan.

Wunderle and Ewert would like to see a Kirtland's warbler habitat plan put into practice, but the number-one obstacle to setting aside or managing land in the Bahamas is the unusual landownership laws. The laws establish four different types of land.

> crown land, which is publicly owned, some of which is held in the form of parks

private land

commonage, which is owned and managed collectively by communities

generational land, which is not necessarily owned but has been occupied by a family since the end of slavery in the Bahamas in the early nineteenth century.

It's the commonage and generational land that make life complicated for a conservationist. Even though commonage land is owned and managed collectively by a community, it can become private land if an individual decides he wants to own it and can demonstrate he can care for it—which is exactly what happened on the team's Rock Sound site. Several plants in the team's phenology study were scheduled to be removed by the man who is maintaining the plot with the intent to take ownership. Wunderle, however, persuaded the man not to cut the plants until after the study was concluded in exchange for a case of the man's favorite beer, Guinness stout. The cost of that beer, Wunderle says, came out of his own pocket.

Ownership of generational land is even muddier. Even though individuals or families may have occupied a piece of land for two hundred years, they may not necessarily own it. The people who occupy generational land have a claim on it, but the land can be taken away from them if it is not used or at least maintained. Kirtland's warblers are often found on generational land because the vegetation is regularly disturbed—bulldozed or cleared by fire—as the people who occupy the land demonstrate that they are "maintaining" it. Wunderle says it's these owners who eye the Kirtland's warbler team most suspiciously and approach to ask if they are surveyors. And even though Wunderle and Ewert do their best to assure the occupants they are they are only scientists searching for a bird, it's often not good enough. Wunderle says he has seen a pattern of land being bulldozed shortly after his team has visited a site. He also admits the cynic in him says that to ensure that good Kirtland's warbler habitat is regularly created, he should visit overgrown plots of generational land on a five-year cycle to ensure regular disturbances.

Almost none of the land on Eleuthera is crown land, so there's no room for a national park or nature preserve. That means that Wunderle and Ewert need to work either with the owners of private land—like the man who owns the Goat Farm—or with commonage committees.

It's not enough just to find Kirtland's warblers and follow them around Eleuthera. Ewert and Wunderle want to understand why the birds are there and what attracts them to specific spots on this specific island. The key to answering that question is to determine what the Kirtland's warbler eats, how its diet changes from fall to spring, and what happens to the food over the course of a winter as rainfall declines and heat increases in February, March, and April. So the team needs to determine exactly what the Kirtland's warbler eats and then estimate its abundance.

Once the mist nets are set up at the Goat Farm, the team busies itself counting berries. It became apparent to Wunderle and Ewert early on in this study that Kirtland's warblers depend on both invertebrates and the fruit of wild sage, black torch, and snowberry. So three times over the course of the winter the team counts all the berries on selected plants or plants found on transects on their study sites. Over the course of this particular winter, the team has counted well over a million berries on the various bushes. Wunderle says he has never seen such a banner year for snowberry.

"There will be a recognition and a celebration for the things that these people have gone through. And they *have* suffered," Wunderle says.

The sun is now just minutes from setting on the Goat Farm, but the team is still hard at work. The wind has died down to an occasional puff, and thick-billed vireos still chatter back and forth. Soon it will be too dark to see, but the team members will put lamps on their foreheads and count until they have finished walking their transects. The goal behind counting fruit is to track how the community changes as fall turns to winter and winter turns to spring. Is there food for the birds? Counting berries is a tedious job, but it's critically important because it's an accurate indicator of how much food is available at each site. The other reason it's important is to better understand how often the wild sage produces fruit. Very little research has been conducted on these plants, and their cycles are poorly understood.

The one thing all the study sites have in common is that they are rich in fruit. The team has learned that an abundance of sage, black torch, and snowberry plants at a location is the best predictor that a Kirtland's warbler will be wintering in the area. To get a better understanding of how these sites developed, Wunderle and his collaborators plan to study more than twenty years of satellite images of Eleuthera, which will allow the team to determine when the areas were disturbed so they can follow the vegetation as it changes. That information will help them determine how long it takes for the vegetation to recover from a disturbance and how long the vegetation is in a state that is attractive to the warbler.

Other than drought, there are few natural threats to the Kirtland's warbler on Eleuthera. There are boas and falcons, but Wunderle doesn't think either predator captures many Kirtland's warblers. Surprisingly, however, there may be human predators. Any small, generally brown bird is known to Bahamians as a "chimmey," and there is a culture on some other Caribbean islands of catching, killing, stripping, cooking, and eating these birds. But Wunderle says he does not worry about losing Kirtland's warblers to human consumption in the Bahamas because eating small birds is not part of the culture or the diet. On some of the other islands in the West Indies, particularly those whose cultures grew out of French colonial rule, small birds need to be constantly on the lookout.

The biggest threat to the Kirtland's warbler might be feral cats. As part of the effort to follow the movements of warblers from fall through spring, team members have mounted tiny radio transmitters on several birds. The radio is extremely light and small and designed to fall off the bird after about three weeks. Once, when team members had determined that a transmitter mounted on one bird had stopped moving, they guessed it had fallen off the bird and conducted a search to recover it for use on another. They found the transmitter, but unfortunately they also found a pile of feathers.

The loss of a single bird to a predator is no longer as great a loss to the entire population as it used to be. Still, a loss is a loss, and when asked if he ever gets emotionally attached to his study subjects Wunderle pauses and ponders not what to say but whether to be honest.

"I'm not supposed to say this, but when I see a bird come back the following fall . . ." He quickly changes the subject to his memories of a Kirtland's warbler that was known as "the Michigan Bird." This particular bird had been banded many years earlier in Michigan, so many years earlier, in fact, that the color had faded from its three plastic bands. The only way Wunderle and his team could identify this bird was to capture it and read the code on the aluminum band. Wunderle admits he was disappointed the year it did not return to Eleuthera.

(Wunderle is not alone in his affection for a specific Kirtland's warbler. In 1983, research biologist Paul Sykes caught and banded a Kirtland's warbler near Governor's Harbour on Eleuthera. Because of this, Sykes referred to this bird as "the Governor." A few months after banding it on Eleuthera, Sykes and Mike Petrucha caught the bird in Michigan, and Sykes was able to catch it in each of the two subsequent years. Sykes admits a special bond with the Governor and was disappointed the following summer when the bird did not return to Michigan.)

Even though there aren't many threats for a Kirtland's warbler now, Ewert sees a large threat looming in the form of invasive plants. Already common on Eleuthera are Brazilian pepper, a vine that covers and eventually smothers the bushes and plants underneath, and jumbie bean, a tree species from Africa that if not controlled will eventually monopolize an area.

Fieldwork on Eleuthera is a seven-days-a-week operation and highly structured. The team is up and out the door before dawn every day, and the morning's work is usually completed by 10:00 a.m., although sometimes it can go as late as noon. The afternoon is a time for lunch, a shower, a nap, a check on e-mail, or work on side projects before heading out into the field again at 4:00. The day usually concludes around sunset but sometimes can go well after dark. Mosquitoes are often a problem, as are the Bahamas' version of no-see-ums. Although there is no poison ivy, Wunderle can speak from experience how miserable contact with poisonwood can be. Early on in the project, he contracted a bad rash from poisonwood while clearing vegetation on a study site. Even though he was careful enough to never let the plant touch his bare skin, his pants wicked up enough of the oil from the plant to cause a terrible rash on his thighs and across his groin.

Pretty much the only other threat comes from wasps and spiders. Besides tarantulas, black widow spiders are found at each of the study sites. Team members always take extra care when moving rocks just in case one is hiding underneath. And where there are tarantulas, there are tarantula hawks, a wasp species said to have one of the most painful stings of any insect. Luckily for the team, this wasp is not aggressive toward humans. While standing on Madeira Road one day, Wunderle actually had a wasp try to hide a paralyzed tarantula under his shoe.

There's not much to Tarpum Bay, and nobody will confuse it with Governor's Harbour, the winter playground for wealthy Americans a few miles to the north. The few snowbirds and tourists who leave their resorts and condos to explore Eleuthera usually drive right through Tarpum Bay, barely slowing down to make the sharp turn where the Queen's Highway turns away from the coast and heads uphill and south toward Rock Sound. There is some agriculture in the area, and Tarpum Bay has a few shops, grocery stores, and restaurants, but there are few jobs, and ambitious young people often head to Nassau for jobs or school.

In the nineteenth century Tarpum Bay was an export center for pineapples, and the area thrived until the pineapple industry collapsed when Floridians started growing pineapples for themselves. With pineapples no longer in demand, farmers shifted to citrus, only to have that industry fail because of poor soil and winter drought. Today's economy revolves around conch, which is sold at roadside stands and in restaurants and is eaten fried, breaded and fried, and raw in salads.

A visitor wandering the streets of Tarpum Bay finds it easy to get into a conversation in a grocery store or an impromptu game of catch with some of the neighborhood boys. It's tough, however, to find your way around town because there are no addresses on the buildings and street signs are rare. If a loved one wanted to mail a letter or a care package to a family member working on the Kirtland's warbler team, the only address needed would be

The Bird House
Tarpum Bay
Eleuthera
Bahamas

Everybody in Tarpum Bay knows the Bird House. It's a two-story, concrete building, painted white, with a waist-high green concrete wall along the street. The local kids come in without knocking just to say hi and nose around. Several stray dogs have adopted the residents, hanging around outside, under the shade of a banana tree, waiting for team members to come out and bring them a treat or offer a scratch behind the ears. Although there is a small porch and the weather can be inviting, no one works outside because they would be unable to get anything done. Sitting on the porch is an invitation for passersby to stop and chat.

There is no television in the Bird House, but there is wireless high-speed Internet, which team members use for research data transmission, as well as to keep in touch with friends and relatives, look for jobs, and maintain a flow of work. The sound of fingers on keyboards is pretty much constant.

On warm afternoons, there is a steady breeze blowing through the trees outside and through the windows. The rustling of the palm fronds and the breeze induce a state of drowsiness that is the cause of another occupational hazard of fieldwork there—the much dreaded "keyboard face." It's the condition you get from falling asleep while working at your computer. When you wake up, you discover you have used your open laptop as a pillow and the keys have left their imprint on your face. Luckily, it's a temporary condition.

There are four bedrooms in the Bird House—two up and two down. Wunderle and Johnson each get one to themselves on the first floor, which leaves two bedrooms for four women upstairs. Between the upstairs bedrooms is a common area, with a couple of chairs and couches and a long makeshift desk that can handle three people at once. With all the sleeping areas otherwise claimed, Ewert gets a couch in the common area when he visits. Despite the close quarters, there have never been any big fights or blowups.

The Bird House is a cluttered place with a severe lack of closet and storage space, but everything has found a place over the years, even if it never really gets put away. Cereal boxes line the kitchen counter and the top of the refrigerator. Plastic shelving holds walkie-talkies and field equipment. A centrifuge used for separating blood is stored on the floor in the common area because there is no other place for it. Anyone passing through the common area needs to tread carefully so as not to trip on the several power cables that crisscross the floor to power the various laptops and printers. Everyone is respectful of others' space and emotions.

It's yet another morning of fieldwork, but the residents of the Bird House are stirring later than usual today. They have the luxury of sleeping in a bit because the first stop of the morning is just outside of town, an area of wells that supply drinking water for Tarpum Bay. The team has found two Kirtland's warblers in this field in the past. Given the generally poor quality of the food supply, the team is returning here in hopes of finding a bird so they can check its health by measuring its weight and taking a feather to determine its diet.

Because the team visits this spot only sporadically, members carry everything they need. Elise Corliss leads the team, carrying a tape player that broadcasts Kirtland's warbler songs. Jen Thieme lags behind, carrying the mist net and poles. They are not heavy, but they are bulky. The poles are eight feet long, which makes it difficult for Thieme to move around without whacking a bush, tree, or coworker. Jen White carries the banding gear. Wunderle and Ewert trail about twenty yards behind in case a Kirtland's reacts to the recorded call somewhat late. If the team members find a bird, they will turn off the tape player, drop everything, quickly set up the net, turn the tape player on again under the net, and hope that the bird will fly into the net as it defends its territory from the taped intruder. The team developed this technique while working at the Madeira Road site during the second year of the study. Unable to enter the study site after the land dispute began, the team kept tabs on it from the middle of Madeira Road. On one visit, they found an unbanded male Kirtland's warbler that was very responsive to the taped song. Given this bird's aggressive behavior, they decided to ignore everything they had learned about how to net a bird—setting up and anchoring a net, then scrambling to hide so as not to drive off the bird with their presence. Instead, Wunderle, Currie, and Leno Davis, then a student at the College of the Bahamas, stretched a twelve-meter net down the middle of the road with Currie and Davis holding poles on either side in plain view. Wunderle put the speaker under the net and then sat out in the open to run the tape player. Within seconds, the warbler was in the net. The experience made Wunderle realize that speed was more important than hiding.

After marching around the well field for a couple of hours without finding any indication that Kirtland's warblers are still there, the decision is made to call it a morning. On the way out, Wunderle points out a snowberry plant, and it is easy to see why a Kirtland's warbler might leave this location in favor of a better one. The fruit on the snowberry hangs limp and black after having been plump and bright white just a few weeks earlier.

"Now we understand many of the drivers of their movements," Wunderle says.

With the close of this year's field season, the heavy science work has been completed. The next phase is to develop and institute a habitat management plan. The first questions Wunderle and Ewert want to answer is what is the best way to maintain current habitat and create new habitat from scratch. Once they answer those questions they will write habitat guidelines for the coppice and hope and pray that they will not be ignored.

"Libraries are filled with all sorts of information on conservation that goes nowhere," Wunderle says. "I would be pleased to see what we have found actually applied here."

Finally, they will create an education program that will help residents of Eleuthera understand why it's important to maintain young coppice. Wunderle admits he would be pleased to see the Kirtland's warbler conservation effort taken over by goat farmers.

Ewert and Wunderle stress that the team's experience on Eleuthera provides insight into the Kirtland's warbler's life in this one small part of the Bahamas only, and it would be wrong to reach broad conclusions about the warbler's winter needs from what they have learned here. The islands of the Bahamas stretch more than four hundred miles and cover more than five thousand square miles, and there is tremendous variation in the vegetation and climate across that range. There are likely conditions—such as fire—that exist on those islands that might have an impact on Kirtland's warbler habitat that the researchers haven't considered because they haven't yet been encountered.

Nevertheless, the team's work has to be considered a success for a couple of reasons. First, they discovered that Kirtland's warblers prefer berry-rich coppice and they banded more than 225 birds. Because of their work, future researchers will now know exactly where they can find the warblers, unlike many who came before and spent much of their time searching in pine habitats. The idea that Kirtland's warblers were more likely to be found in pine grew out of a paper published in the *Condor* in 1998 that made a quantitative analysis of winter sight records dating back to 1841.[6] That analysis found no evidence to support previous claims that "Kirtland's Warblers prefer scrub or avoid pine habitats." The study concluded that Kirtland's warblers were detected in the pine woodlands of Abaco and Grand Bahama islands more frequently than other habitats. That analysis seemed to become conventional wisdom and perhaps had the effect of throwing the bloodhounds off the scent.

Second, Wunderle and Ewert had the luxury of good timing. In the twenty years since Sykes's work on Eleuthera, the Kirtland's warbler population had tripled, and this new team was looking for a species whose population was considerably larger than it was when any of the other researchers were tromping through the islands. Even though Ewert and Wunderle were searching the same haystack, thanks to successful habitat management by the Kirtland's Warbler Recovery Team on the nesting grounds, there are a lot more needles now.

TEN : Inspiring a New Generation of Conservationists

Ancilleno "Leno" Davis remembers exactly where he was the day the Kirtland's warbler changed his life. It was in 2001, and Davis, a student at the College of the Bahamas, was visiting the Nassau Botanical Gardens for a project in his vertebrate biology class. That's when he met Eric Carey.

Carey, who would go on to become the executive director of the Bahamas National Trust, was working at the botanical gardens at the time and was actively searching for a student to work with David Ewert and Joe Wunderle in the Kirtland's Warbler Research and Training Project. Carey was immediately impressed with Davis's curiosity and above average knowledge and knew right away that he would be a good addition to the team. Mincing no words, Carey unequivocally told Davis that he needed to do something with his life—and offered an opportunity. If Davis would spend a field season with the Kirtland's Warbler Research and Training Project, The Nature Conservancy would provide him with a scholarship to a college in the United States. But there was one important provision: if he accepted the scholarship he must return to the Bahamas after graduation and use his education to work to preserve and protect his country's natural resources.

Not only would Davis be paid to spend time in the bush learning about Bahamian ecosystems and the animals that inhabit them, he would get a chance to obtain an advanced degree. He jumped at the chance and became the first of nine students to join the Kirtland's Warbler Research and Training Project.

Wunderle and Ewert could have called their project the Kirtland's Warbler Research Project because the single most important goal was to document the Kirtland's warbler's habitat requirements in the Bahamas. But the two experienced scientists knew that if they wanted the findings of their research to be applied in ways that would benefit the Kirtland's warbler they would also need to find people to perform additional research and work to protect and maintain the warbler's habitat. With few Bahamians possessing those skills, Ewert and Wunderle would need to find students and train them.

Besides participating in fieldwork with the team, each of the students that joined the team traveled to Michigan to participate in the annual Kirtland's warbler census in early June and to spend time working with professional wildlife biologists on the bird's nesting grounds.

Davis admits that he knew nothing about the Kirtland's warbler when he joined the project and the only birds he could identify were a gull, a pigeon, and a chicken. He quickly mastered a crash course in bird identification, learning the field marks, songs, and calls of many Bahamian birds in just thirty days.

When the Bahamian field season finished, Davis traveled with Ewert to Michigan to further learn about the Kirtland's warbler and search for colleges. He chose the University of Maryland Eastern Shore and received both his bachelor's and master's degrees before returning to work in the Bahamas as a conservation coordinator with the Nature Conservancy in Nassau. In his job, Davis is responsible for helping to educate his fellow Bahamians as to why it is important to save the nation's natural areas and prevent the spread of invasive species such as the lionfish and *Casuarina,* an evergreen from Australia and Asia.

Davis says that because the Bahamas is more like a small, close-knit community than a big, diverse nation, the best way to spread his message is at the grassroots level. Davis started his educational effort by giving a presentation to a Rotary Club meeting that was attended by bankers and other business leaders, the president of the Bahamas Scouting Association, and schoolteachers. People attending that meeting invited Davis to speak to other groups, and people in attendance at those presentations invited him to speak to yet more organizations.

After a couple of appearances on local television, people began to recognize Davis on the street.

"In general, people do love the Bahamas, they do love how beautiful it is, the fish and the coral reefs and the birds," Davis said. "But a lot of Bahamians don't really know about it sufficiently to protect it."

Eleanor Phillips, the director of the Nature Conservancy's Northern Caribbean Program, believes that the training aspect of the Kirtland's warbler project will have a positive long-term impact on the Bahamas. She admits that a lack of scientists has kept her country from developing a stronger environmental consciousness and setting aside sensitive areas, and that Davis and the other students coming out of the Kirtland's warbler project is exactly what her country needs. Phillips says she is already seeing the result of Davis's work in grade-school classrooms across the country. Children are becoming more interested in conservation and environmental issues and excited about learning more about the nation's wildlife.

More important, Phillips said, children are seeing a role model in Davis—a professional scientist who is successful, making money, and enjoying his work.

Even though Davis now works for the Nature Conservancy, he keeps his eyes open for Kirtland's warblers during his travels around the Bahamas. In the winter of 2009, he unexpectedly found two Kirtland's warblers on Exuma Cay.

"If you find a Kirtland's by yourself, that's like the most dubious record ever," Davis said. "Luckily, I had my camera with me. . . . I got some excellent photos of a Kirtland's just gleaning off some *Strumpfia maritima* over there. . . . And then, I guess maybe an hour later, another Kirtland's comes chipping, and I got video of it. . . . So this has caused a big hullabaloo inside the birding world. Of course, there are people who are, like, 'No, you didn't see a Kirtland's.' Anyone can see a Kirtland's by himself, but I've got images to prove it. So lucky for me I had a camera with me that day."

"And," he added, "I'll tell you that the excitement of finding a Kirtland's doesn't really diminish."

The old-timers now look back and laugh.

Like any good story, some facts have become stretched, changed, lost, or enhanced over the years, but what happened on June 17, 1985, will live in Kirtland's warbler legend. On gathering the "facts" from various sources, a dramatic story emerges in which a single heroic Michigan Department of Natural Resources conservation officer faced down a column of Ohio National Guard tanks driving through prime Kirtland's warbler nesting habitat near Camp Grayling, the Michigan National Guard's largest base, and ordered them to halt.

The conservation officer then arrested the unit's commanding officer and put him in jail.

A few days later, legend has it, a photo of the conservation officer's vehicle, nose-to-nose with the tanks, ran in the local weekly newspaper.

According to court records, however, the truth is a bit less sexy. Responding to a citizen's complaint, Bruce Patrick, a state conservation officer, drove to a remote spot in Crawford County where he found nine M60 tanks stopped on a dirt road. The tanks had got lost on maneuvers and strayed outside the border of the base. They had just driven through a stand of young jack pine and stopped directly between two "Area Closed" signs when Patrick found them.

Patrick ticketed Charles Edward Holwerda, a lieutenant in the Michigan National Guard and the unit's commanding officer, for "operating a vehicle/entering a Kirtland's warbler area." Holwerda admitted to Patrick that he had been briefed on staying out of the Kirtland's warbler nesting areas and even had a map clearly showing the areas to avoid. He also admitted that he had simply got lost in the thick trees.

Four days later the officers' fund of Holwerda's unit paid fines and court costs of $105.00, and the issue was resolved. No Kirtland's warbler nests were destroyed or damaged by the tanks, and no one has ever been able to produce a photo of the incident.

The ticket issued to Holwerda was not the first time that the DNR and Michigan National Guard had clashed over the Kirtland's warbler. It did, however, mark the lowest point in the relationship between the two organizations. In the early 1970s, the DNR had angered National Guard commanders by ordering vast areas of Kirtland's warbler nesting grounds on Camp Grayling property off-limits to training from May 1 through August 1 because of large numbers of nesting Kirtland's warblers. In 1971 alone, the Kirtland's warbler census found 30 percent of the singing males were on the base's tank range. The DNR's power over the National Guard was further enhanced by the passage of the Endangered Species Act in 1973, which stipulated that the military was no longer exempt from environmental laws.

The DNR believed it had a responsibility to protect the Kirtland's warbler, and the military, like it or not, wasn't going to interfere. If that meant also restricting Air National Guard training flights near occupied Kirtland's warbler habitat in Iosco and Alcona counties, then so be it.

"Those were heady times," Jerry Weinrich, the retired Michigan DNR wildlife biologist, said with a big grin of satisfaction. "The people at the Michigan National Guard did not believe that we could or would claim certain areas of Camp Grayling as off-limits because of the Kirtland's warbler, but that's what we did."

National Guard commanders angrily objected to the DNR intruding on their base and compromising their training—especially while the United States was embroiled in the Vietnam War and the cold war and widespread social discontent was flaring at home. In addition, the Michigan National Guard was also hearing complaints from the out-of-state units that annually ventured north to Camp Graying to train.

Units from Ohio and Indiana were asking why they should come all the way to Camp Grayling to be told they could use only a portion of the facility.

When it came to the Kirtland's warbler, however, the Michigan National Guard was inadvertently setting out the welcome mat. The use of smoke pots and live fire from helicopter gunships and artillery regularly caused forest fires in the jack pine. And that meant that the guard was unintentionally creating new Kirtland's warbler nesting habitat. In fact, fires set by the National Guard created more habitat than anything the DNR or the U.S. Forest Service was doing at the time.

Frustration with the bird led one of the base's commanding officers to give the Kirtland's warbler a nickname: FLAW, which stood for feathered lightweight antitank weapon. But facing the annual closure of thousands of acres and the embarrassment of a unit commander being ticketed, the National Guard sued for peace.

Land use conflicts dominate the history of endangered species protection in the United States. In the late 1980s, loggers in Oregon claimed that thousands of jobs would be lost if they were unable to harvest vast old-growth forests that were home to an endangered subspecies of the spotted owl. The discovery of the snail darter in the Little Tennessee River in 1973 temporarily halted the construction of a hydroelectric dam. It took an act of Congress to exempt the dam's owner from the Endangered Species Act. A landowner in North Carolina, who had been managing forest on his land for several different wildlife species, decided to cut down trees on his land rather than allow them to grow old enough to support the nesting of the red-cockaded woodpecker. The landowner feared that once the woodpecker became established on his land he would not be able to manage it the way he wanted because once an endangered species is found on private property, the property owner is required by law to meet the protection demands of U.S. Fish and Wildlife Service biologists.

Unlike some of the more notorious conflicts involving endangered species, the Kirtland's warbler never stopped logging or halted a construction project, and it has never been the cause of a lawsuit. There are two reasons why the agencies managing for the Kirtland's warbler have avoided a protracted court fight. First, conflicts have been few because the Kirtland's warbler's primary habitat in northern lower Michigan is on public land; therefore it has had very little impact on private land. Second, members of the Kirtland's Warbler Recovery Team and the various agencies have learned since the Mack Lake fire that sometimes the best solution to a conflict is to gather everybody in a room and talk things out—which is exactly how the problem with the Michigan National Guard was solved.

With the National Guard losing the battle over the use of its own facility, in 1983 its adjutant general requested that Greg Huntington, the chief of its environmental division, be appointed to the Kirtland's Warbler Recovery Team as an ex-officio member. Huntington immediately started a conversation with the DNR, and soon he was spending time in the field, learning about the Kirtland's warbler and building relationships with wildlife biologists and foresters. Before long, Huntington and the biologists began to understand each other.

"They shared with me what they felt was important for them, and I shared the military's interests," Huntington said. "Over the years, we realized that we each could probably give some."

Although Huntington was talking with all the members of the recovery team, he worked with the Michigan DNR directly and formed a sense of trust with Raymond Perez and Jerry Weinrich. That trust allowed the DNR and the guard to begin to search for solutions.

Perez was intimately familiar with the base because he was also responsible for keeping tabs on the sharp-tailed grouse population, and the craters and lack of vegetation on the bombing range made it a great mating ground for the species each spring. So on spring mornings, he would arrive on the range before sunrise and lie down in a crater to watch and count the grouse as they performed their mating dances all around him. Both Perez and the grouse made certain they were out of the area by 9:00 a.m., which is when the bombs began to fall.

The first nesting location Perez started discussing with Huntington was Bucks Crossing, an area smack dab in the middle of the base's tank range, which was both densely populated with Kirtland's warblers and used intensively for military training. Unfortunately, there was concern that Bucks Crossing was potentially filled with unexploded ammunition and tank rounds, which would make it impossible for the DNR to clear-cut and replant trees for the warbler. So Perez and Huntington turned their attention to a smaller area on the eastern edge of the base, Bald Hill. This area also had a dense Kirtland's warbler population with good habitat as a result of a May 10, 1975, fire sparked by tank practice, which burned more than four thousand acres on and off the base. Six years after the fire, the warblers moved in. And, like Mack Lake, the area of the Bald Hill fire featured a two-tiered elevation that would keep the habitat viable for a longer period.

As a result of talks, the Michigan Department of Military Affairs agreed to let the DNR manage Bald Hill for Kirtland's warblers. In exchange, the DNR would not force the National Guard to do any Kirtland's warbler management on any other part of the base. Furthermore, if new fires occurred and Kirtland's warbler nesting habitat started to develop, the military had the option of removing the habitat before it was old enough to be occupied.

The 1986 agreement between the DNR and the National Guard was innovative in that it was a forerunner to the "safe harbor" concept developed by the U.S. Fish and Wildlife Service in the mid-1990s. A safe harbor agreement assures a landowner who agrees to carry out activities expected to benefit an endangered species that no additional Endangered Species Act restrictions will be imposed on the landowner as a result of his or her management work. Furthermore, a safe harbor agreement essentially freezes a landowner's Endangered Species Act responsibilities at their current levels for a particular species if he or she agrees to restore, enhance, or create habitat for that species.[1]

Even though the National Guard's attitude toward the Kirtland's warbler and other endangered and threatened species has changed 180 degrees since the 1970s and early 1980s, the bird's future impact on Camp Grayling will be minimal because the National Guard does a good job fighting fires and the few areas of jack pine that accidentally burn will typically not be large enough to support a colony.

The Bald Hill agreement established a rapprochement that led to a second agreement, hammered out between Huntington and Weinrich in 2006, which allows the military to camp and perform maneuvers in Kirtland's warbler nesting areas but prevents it from using heavy equipment or firing live ammunition in those areas.

Although the National Guard still doesn't like the idea of having its training compromised by the presence of the Kirtland's warbler, it has come to accept and accommodate the endangered warbler and the two species found on the base that are classified as threatened, the eastern massasauga rattlesnake and Houghton's goldenrod.

"We both knew that we couldn't succeed without compromising," said Perez. "There was a lot of hard work, a lot of communication, a lot of soul-searching. . . . Had we not had that sense of understanding, we would still be arguing, maybe even today."

The DNR had the authority to close vast areas of Camp Grayling each nesting season because when it comes to protecting an endangered species the law is clear. Drafting and implementing a recovery plan, however, can be messy and rife with politics because, instead of creating a closed process in which policy is made within the U.S. Fish and Wildlife Service exclusively, section 4 of the Endangered Species Act allows for federal agencies to create recovery teams to develop species recovery plans and sometimes even implement them. The recovery team provision created an open process that allows field biologists, politicians, special interest groups, and just plain citizens to give their input. Given that all these individuals and groups may have conflicting goals or turf or budgets to protect, it is easy for the work of a recovery team to get bogged down in acrimony.

The Kirtland's Warbler Recovery Team, however, is an example of the way the process should work. It was established in 1975, growing out of the advisory committee that was established in Ann Arbor in October 1971. Like other recovery teams, the Kirtland's warbler team has no actual power and does not make policy. But it does have considerable influence with policymakers at the DNR, the U.S. Forest Service, and the U.S. Fish and Wildlife Service. That influence has grown out of a track record of success, a history of cooperation and accommodation that is unusual, and a desire to hold the team together not just to guide a recovery but to plan for the distant future.

John Byelich, a wildlife biologist with the Michigan DNR, was chosen as the recovery team's first leader because he was respected as a soft-spoken, "work in the trenches" kind of guy who understood the issues surrounding the Kirtland's warbler better than anyone else. As team leader, Byelich immediately put his stamp on the committee by assigning different members of the team to write the various sections of the first recovery plan, a move that limited acrimony because it gave everybody a stake in process—and established the culture of cooperation that has guided the recovery team's efforts for more than thirty years.

"We'd have a meeting, go home and write it up, come back together, and everybody would have a crack at reviewing it," Bill Irvine said. "It was a group effort. John just kept us working at it."

Byelich's folksy demeanor and ability to relate and communicate kept everyone focused and the process moving forward, but, Irvine said, everyone on the team shared Byelich's determination. "It wasn't just a job, it was a passion," he said. "We were deadly serious about it. . . . We looked at this bird as being an important part of the fabric of the jack pine forest, and if we didn't do something, then we should have our butts kicked."

There were conflicts and disagreements in those early days, but none allowed the process to bog down. The earliest recovery team members argued over whether to allow researchers into the nesting areas and whether those researchers should be allowed to touch the young birds in order to band them. Once that issue was settled in favor of allowing research, the team tussled over how much habitat each agency—the DNR or the Forest Service—would create. And after that they discussed why the population wasn't growing. Some said the problem was lack of suitable habitat in Michigan, others said there was some unidentified problem on the wintering grounds, and some wondered if the birds were getting lost in migration.

And then there was Paul Aird's personal research project. Aird, an emeritus professor of forestry at the University of Toronto, is a mild-mannered gentleman, but in the late 1980s he raised new questions that got the recovery team's attention.

Although Aird had never seen a Kirtland's warbler, he used the species' habitat needs to illustrate forest management issues in his lectures and public speeches. In 1974, he decided to catalog Kirtland's warbler's sightings in Ontario. Once Aird completed the list, he discovered something curious: only one of the sightings was in jack pine habitat. Had no one ever searched for Kirtland's warblers nesting in the jack pine forests of Ontario? Knowing an area that was potentially fine nesting habitat on Canadian Forces Base Petawawa, just east of Algonquin Provincial Park, Aird blithely set off in 1977 to search for the Kirtland's warbler. To his surprise, it didn't take long. Using a taped Kirtland's warbler song, it took only minutes on his first morning of searching to find a singing male.

Excitedly, Aird immediately called several colleagues, including members of the Royal Ontario Museum and the University of Toronto, and invited them up to see the bird. Unfortunately, the group searched for three straight days without luck. On the seventh day—with all his colleagues gone—Aird once again found the male in the same habitat where he originally found it. He later discovered that his male had two territories a half mile apart.

Even though there was just one bird, the sighting was important enough to lure Byelich and Lawrence Walkinshaw to the area. Walkinshaw banded the male and noted that the habitat was similar to Michigan's in its patchy mosaic.

Meanwhile, back in Michigan, some members of the recovery team were skeptical of Aird's sightings. Nest in Ontario? Why should any effort be wasted on one bird that had been found so far away? Aird recalls being told that the Ontario bird was there only because a tornado blew it off course. Others told Aird that the bird was there by accident and would soon find its way back to Michigan.

But it didn't. Not only did Aird watch this bird for five weeks before ending his search for the year, but the following year he found the same male in the same two territories. Aird says that at the time he marveled at how a bird could migrate from Ontario to the Bahamas and return the next year to the same trees in Ontario. It could only be, he thought, because the bird possessed an internal compass.

Also in 1978, Aird found a lonely male in Quebec and soon determined that these birds weren't there by accident; they were there because this was part of the warbler's natural range. Aird's argument was bolstered when the recovery team learned that a male warbler was found in Wisconsin in 1978 that had been banded by Walkinshaw as a nestling six years earlier.

At a 1989 symposium on the Kirtland's warbler in Lansing, Michigan, Aird publicly offered his hypothesis: "Since the jack pine habitat of the Kirtland's warbler may be suitable for nesting for only about 20 years, the dispersal of the Kirtland's warbler to establish new nesting grounds, beyond the known Michigan center, must be inherent in the species and evident in its behavior."[2]

Aird's hypothesis that the Kirtland's warbler brain is wired to constantly seek out new nesting grounds is not universally shared by all wildlife biologists, but some agree that his theory helps to explain the warbler's recent expansion into Wisconsin and Ontario. Considering that the birds jump over the Gulf Stream to get from the Bahamas to the North American continent and back again, a postnesting flight across Lake Michigan or Lake Huron isn't all that big a deal. Then again, ornithologists have shown that a small percentage of the birds hatched every year are born unable to home precisely. That homing deficiency could explain the tiny number of birds in Ontario.

Aird admits that he had a second reason for exploding the myth that the Kirtland's nested only in Michigan: If that population succumbed to some tragedy and went extinct, there was the possibility, based on these sightings, that a second nesting population existed someplace in eastern Ontario or western Quebec, and steps should be taken immediately to find this population and preserve it. Heeding Aird's concern, the Kirtland's warbler was declared an endangered species in Canada in 1979, based on the belief that the species once nested in the region as documented at the Petawawa Military Camp northwest of Ottawa, Ontario, in 1916, 1939, 1946, 1977, and 1978.

Although nesting was never confirmed, it appears that the Kirtland's warbler may have been a well-established resident in eastern Ontario in the early twentieth century. Paul Harrington, a Canadian military dentist who was also a bird-watcher and egg collector, wrote in the *Jack-Pine Warbler* that the birds were "not uncommon" on what was then Petawawa in 1916.[3] Harrington, with his fellow medical professional, Dr. F. A. Starr, reported seeing and hearing several Kirtland's warblers in the area, and even though they could not confirm it, they felt sure the birds nested in the area. In that same issue of the *Jack-Pine Warbler*, Walkinshaw optimistically predicted that the Kirtland's warbler would one day be documented nesting outside of Michigan.

> If one glances over a map of North America and notes the wide fan-like area covered in the northern part of the species migration range, he immediately sees that the species does not concentrate toward Michigan but spreads from Minnesota to Ontario. It seems logical that it will eventually be found in Ontario, Wisconsin and possibly Minnesota breeding. I have spent many hours in the jack pine areas of north central Wisconsin during late June but thus far have been unable to find the species there. However, I do not feel that it is not there and expect some day to hear or read that it has been found breeding in Wisconsin.[4]

In 1939, Harrington went back to Petawawa and spent three days looking for Kirtland's warblers. He was unable to make a complete survey because of constant artillery practice, but on June 5, as Harrington was resting in the shade of a pine tree, a Kirtland's warbler landed on a nearby limb and stayed in view for several minutes.

In 2006, a Canadian Forces research team composed of Tammy Richard, Nancy Hiscock, and Aird found two male Kirtland's warblers on the base, and in 2007 Richard, the base biologist, found a pair of Kirtland's warblers nesting on Canadian Forces Base Petawawa. After the nesting was completed, the nest and an unviable egg were collected and donated to the Royal Ontario Museum in Toronto.

Even though the Kirtland's warbler now nests in Ontario, Canadian birders will still likely have to go to Michigan to see it, as CFB Petawawa is closed to outsiders.

Although Aird's search for the Kirtland's warbler touched off discussion among members of the Kirtland's Warbler Recovery Team, it did not rise to the level of some of the disagreements members of the team have worked through. Surprisingly, Carol Bocetti, the team leader, believes that disagreement and intense debate are a healthy thing because they help everyone to focus on a topic. And, she said, eventually, the best argument will win.

"I have been associated with other recovery teams where sometimes positions are held because egos are in the way," Bocetti said. "It goes all the way down to shared research data. We just do not see that kind of turfing going on in this program." Disputes are settled by "stepping into that uncomfortable place and talking it out—and then everyone goes out to dinner together."

Phil Huber, a wildlife biologist with the U.S. Forest Service in Mio and a member of the recovery team since the early 1990s, agrees that there are disagreements but thinks they are important because they create the collective consciousness that has helped to define a role for each individual and agency.

"If we all thought the same, we wouldn't need each other," Huber said. "We learn from each other. By coming together as a recovery team we developed some common thoughts and changed each other to be about 95 percent on the same page."

Indeed, a meeting of the Kirtland's Warbler Recovery Team is a little like a family reunion crossed with a meeting of policy wonks at a science fair. Although the recovery team consists of only ten or so members, the meeting room often swells to capacity. Other attendees are state and federal employees, members of various Audubon groups, researchers, academics, a professional photographer, and students on internships.

There is warmth around the table and a general respect for each member of the team and his or her opinions. If there are any grudges they do not seem to surface. In a room full of people who have climbed fairly high up their respective career ladders, the lack of ego is remarkable.

In a typical meeting, the team will discuss the effectiveness of various policies and the best way to apply knowledge gained from the latest scientific research. Even though discussions occur between meetings, the meetings themselves provide members with time to chew over topics and exchange ideas. These discussions are not exactly sexy stuff—there is a lot of talk about stand density and carbon levels and rotation schedules—but they address the kinds of nuts-and-bolts issues that are important to understanding the Kirtland's warbler's needs and managing the habitat.

Much of the discussion at any meeting involves assessing the effectiveness of ongoing policies and practices and reviewing short-term plans for the next nesting season. Although some policy suggestions can be implemented immediately, it may be ten years or more before their impact is felt.

Meetings take place twice a year, usually over a two-day period in the late winter and summer. At the end of the first day's meetings there is a dinner, which might just be the highlight of the two-day period because it gives everybody a chance to swap stories, have a few laughs, catch up on friendships, recall members who have moved on or passed, and quietly celebrate the group's achievements. And it is all done very cheaply. Although the recovery team reviews and approves all research on Kirtland's warblers, the team itself has never been able to throw a party or conduct research because it doesn't have any money or a budget of its own.

Bocetti usually puts herself somewhere near the front of the room but she's never really front and center. She runs a relatively loose meeting and allows productive discussions to go on, but she also keeps a close tab on the time.

Bocetti became a voting member of the recovery team in 1998 and was appointed team leader in 2006. She turned down the job of team leader twice before accepting, initially balking for two reasons. First, she knew it would be difficult to carry out her duties from a distance because she lives in Pennsylvania. Second, she believed that because she was not from one of the agencies she might put the team at a disadvantage. As an outsider she wondered whether she lacked the credibility and authority that comes from wearing a government uniform.

Since taking the position of team leader, however, Bocetti has discovered that not being tied to an agency is an advantage. When she is forced to give an occasional scolding or demand that an agency follow through on its commitment to the Kirtland's warbler, her words carry more credibility because they come from someone without affiliation who is acting in the best interests of the species.

Under Bocetti's guidance, the team has gone from performing the duties of a recovery team to behaving more as an interagency problem-solving group. With the Kirtland's warbler's population leveling out at just under four thousand total birds, the group has been able to shift away from focusing on pressing problems to finding long-term solutions. In addition, the recovery team has also increased its interaction and coordination with the state of Wisconsin and province of Ontario now that Kirtland's warblers are nesting in those two jurisdictions.

Bocetti credits two of the previous team leaders for teaching her what she needed to know about running the team. From John Byelich she learned that she needed a vision of what she wanted the team to be and where she wanted the recovery effort to go in the future. And from Rex Ennis she learned to build consensus among people, agencies, and stakeholders and to understand that there are limits to what the recovery team can do and how fast it can do it.

Bocetti said she could have walked away from Kirtland's warbler work years ago to focus on teaching and the other endangered species with which she works, but she stays with this team because of the dedication to the mission she sees in the people sitting around the table.

"And the coolest thing about it is that there are so many agencies and entities—all with their own mandates and priorities," Bocetti said. "And yet when it comes down to it, the right decisions are made."

Despite scrapes with the Michigan National Guard, internal disagreements, and other conflicts that have come and gone over the years, one conflict has been ongoing as a result of the Mack Lake fire, and it does not seem likely that it will be resolved anytime soon. That conflict is over the clear-cutting of the jack pine forests to create new habitat.

What is the best way to manage a state or national forest? What is the best way to manage that forest for an endangered species? Foresters and wildlife biologists are largely in agreement that the best way to manage for the Kirtland's warbler would be to let nature take its course. And if that means allowing vast sections of the forest to burn occasionally, then so be it. At least one study has shown that female Kirtland's warblers prefer naturally burned stands to plantations that have been clear-cut and replanted.[5] And because clear-cuts do not return carbon to the soil in the same way that a fire would, there is some concern about the long-term impact this declining carbon level will have.

Many state and federal foresters who manage the jack pine barrens might prefer to use fire because it is cheaper, quicker, and less labor intensive than clear-cutting. Unfortunately, since Mack Lake, burning large areas has been out of the question, no matter whether the fire is part of a well-planned prescribed burn or an accident; there are too many people living too close to the forest. So the question becomes: what is the best way to manage the forest in the absence of fire? Since fire has been largely relegated to the bottom of the toolbox, forest managers are left with only one other tool: clear-cutting.

Clear-cutting is a practice that is used by both the state and national agencies because in some stands of trees it's the best way to spur new growth that will attract and support wildlife. For example, the state of Michigan clear-cuts aspen on a forty- to fifty-year rotation because that tree species needs full sunshine to thrive. Once cut, new trees will sprout from the old roots, and these young trees will support more than 70 species of mammals and birds—many of which are popular game or wildlife-viewing species. Clear-cuts of aspen, however, are usually limited to one hundred acres or less at a time.

When it comes to jack pine and the Kirtland's warbler, however, clear-cuts are big—starting at 320 acres and going up to 2,000 (or about 3 square miles) at a time. The bigger is better approach began after the Mack Lake fire, when biologists discovered that the warblers really packed into the burn, ignoring smaller nearby tracts. That discovery prompted foresters to shift away from widely scattered 200-acre blocks that attracted fewer than thirty birds to larger tracts that attracted an exponentially larger population. Not only does the evidence suggest that Kirtland's warblers occupy these larger clear-cuts in higher densities, but they also use them for a longer period of time.

Even though the state and federal governments are doing local residents a favor by removing the fire threat that is old-growth jack pine, many residents react angrily to the sight of a clear-cut. Conventional wisdom on clear-cutting among members of the general public is that it's bad for the environment—even if they don't know exactly why.

Because clear-cuts occur on a decades-long rotation, jack pine stands can go for forty or more years untouched. That is long enough for people to get used to living near a mature forest and maybe even starting to think that it will always be there. They are surprised when one day the trucks and heavy equipment move in and a few days later the forest is gone. What's left is shocking, and it's what residents object to the most—a vista of stumps and slash.

Michigan DNR employees say that they commonly field complaints from people who are upset by changes in areas where they like to snowmobile, hike, or hunt, and they often find allies in their state legislators—who like to do things for their constituents because they want to be reelected. The people who seem to complain loudest about clear-cuts, however, are relative newcomers to the area—people who have moved in from southern Michigan and are unfamiliar with long-standing forest management practices. Often these people are retirees who have left the state's urban areas or people who have invested in a summer home on the edge of state or federal land. Michigan DNR employees say even though clear-cutting is a constant effort in different areas, the issue heats up every few years or so. The DNR responds to complaints by holding public meetings to educate people about how the woods change over the years, the theories behind forest management strategies, and how the livelihoods of many area residents depend on the timber industry. After the meeting, the issue pretty much dies down for a while.

Of course, nothing can be done to change the opinions of those people who just don't like the DNR or the Forest Service or those who believe the supervisors of those agencies cut the timber for personal profit.

Even though the Forest Service also clear-cuts sections of the Huron National Forest on behalf of the Kirtland's warbler, employees in the Mio office say they receive fewer complaints than the DNR does because federal rules limit the size of the clear-cuts to 550 acres at a time. The Forest Service has set aside 88,300 acres of the 450,000-acre forest for the Kirtland's warbler. The Forest Service's Phil Huber says that 88,300 acres may sound like a lot for just one species, but only about 20 percent of that is nesting habitat at any one time. That is because management policies include a certain amount of flexibility. For example, if a block is near a subdivision or small town, jack pine won't be planted right up to the property line to create a firebreak.

Once an area is clear-cut to make new Kirtland's warbler nesting habitat and the marketable wood is removed, stumps and slash aren't all that is left. The management plans for both the state and the Forest Service require that several trees—dead or alive—be left standing per acre. Although these trees provide taller branches for the warblers to perch on, they are commonly used by other wildlife in the area. Depending on the characteristics of the area, a pocket of mature trees may be left to act as a buffer around a pond or wetland or left standing to mimic the landscape after a wildfire. After harvesting, a trenching machine digs long furrows six inches deep, a foot wide, and six to seven feet apart. Trenching is necessary because there is a high failure rate for jack pine seedlings planted in unfurrowed ground. The trencher is followed by a crew that hand plants twelve hundred two-year-old saplings per acre. Depending on scheduling, the availability of the furrowing machine, and the availability of trees, the process can be completed over just a few weeks or a couple of years.

The trees themselves are planted in an "opposing wave" pattern created by John Byelich and first used in 1976. The pattern is intended to mimic the erratic pattern of burning and regeneration caused by a wildfire. The result of planting in this pattern is regularly spaced, quarter-acre openings that provide "edge" habitat. This edge habitat is particularly important for the Kirtland's warbler because many females prefer to build their nests along the edge rather than in the thickest part of the forest.

So why not just cut the block and replant it immediately once the habitat is no longer viable? First, the DNR and the Forest Service must let the trees grow for at least thirty years because younger trees are not economically worthwhile to timber companies. (Some young trees are harvested for biofuel to generate electricity, but that is rare.) Second, cutting and replanting on such a short cycle rapidly depletes the few nutrients in the soil. Finally, among the first decisions the recovery team made was to go with a fifty-year rotation to allow the jack pine to reach maturity for animals and plants that need that type of habitat.

Of course, any desire to manage the forest in the most natural way possible—which means allowing it to burn occasionally—sets up a fundamental conflict between forest managers and area residents who want the government to protect their lives and property.

Perhaps the answer is to seek a balance—one that is tilted toward the humans.

"Agency people have to consider the social and political aspects more than the research people do," said Bob Hess.

Unfortunately, this balancing act has created critics who claim that forest managers are creating nothing more than a Kirtland's warbler zoo by maintaining an artificial habitat.

But self-imposed restrictions on burning appear to be ending as foresters and wildlife biologists at the DNR and Forest Service start to rethink and improve fire control methods. That means that prescribed fire may be returning to the jack pine in the future.

Bocetti says she also wants to invite a public discussion about fire as a management tool. Before the public rejects the idea outright, she needs area residents to understand that fire will be used only as a result of some deep soul-searching and the development of new fire containment techniques. Agencies would use prescribed burns only if they adhere to very strict guidelines. The agencies have already agreed that safety for human life and human property is the number-one priority, the Kirtland's warbler is second, and creating habitat in the jack pine barrens is third.

And, Bocetti, said, the agencies must never forget what is first.

"The pendulum swung pretty far after Mack Lake," Bocetti said. "Now it's coming back a little. We've used fire on a limited number of stands. Now we're thinking about using fire a little bit more—when it is right. It is never going to be that fire is our primary tool."

Nevertheless, Bocetti said, it's time to return the landscape to a more natural way of functioning. "Fire has played a huge role in the landscape. That's the first thing that we have to remember. Fire belongs here."

TWELVE : Giving Voice to a Songbird

I am a Kirtland's warbler; I live in jack pine forest.
A special kind of soil is important for us.
We need low busy branches growing just above the ground
To hide our nest which only in the tall grass can be found.

Have you heard
(Have you heard)
 Of a blue-gray bird
(Of a blue-gray bird)
With a yellow, yellow breast?
Twitchy tail
(Twitchy tail)
And a voice that sails
(And a voice that sails)
Loud and clear above the rest!

Scientists aren't the only people who have become enchanted by a blue-gray bird with a yellow, yellow breast and distinctive song. At least three original songs have been written about the Kirtland's warbler's struggle for survival, including the catchy bluegrass tune, "Kirtland's Warbler," by Ken Lonnquist, whose lyrics are printed above.

Lonnquist, a singer-songwriter from Madison, Wisconsin, wrote his song about the Kirtland's warbler as part of a 1995 children's book and audio recording, *A Place at the Fire*. The book is the story of two children, Sam and Emma, who stumble on a meeting of animals in the woods late one night. Each of the animals takes time to talk about what is happening to it and its habitat and to reflect on changes—good and bad—to the environment in the Great Lakes region. One of the animals that speaks to the council is the Kirtland's warbler, and his story is told in the form of Lonnquist's song. Although Lonnquist wrote the song and sings backup vocals, he turned the lead vocals over to Kathy Bero, the author of the book, because he thought the warbler shouldn't have a deep voice.

Knowing that the average third grader's attention span is pretty short, Lonnquist made the song less than two minutes long and gave it a quick pace and lots of energy to reflect the warbler's personality. He also structured the song to have the verses act as the warbler's own voice and the chorus describe the warbler itself. Lonnquist used the call-and-response form for the chorus because kids like to be able to sing along but also because he wanted to reflect how male warblers sing and countersing when on their territories.

Lonnquist was unfamiliar with the Kirtland's warbler before he was asked to help on the book, but he already had several years' experience writing and performing songs about environmental issues for kids. And once he began to learn about the Kirtland's warbler he became a fan.

Ronn Fryer, an Oscoda, Michigan, native who now teaches ninth-grade English in Charlotte, North Carolina, has also written a song about the Kirtland's warbler, but this one is a slower-paced, reggae-tinged tune written from the bird's point of view. The song reflects the challenges the warbler faces in trying to survive, raise a family, dodge predators, and migrate.

> I live in the branches of the Northern Jack Pine
> Along the Au Sable River in the sweet summertime.
> But it's a dangerous life when you're three inches tall
> Between the Blue Jays and squirrels, I'll try to make it til fall.
> Then it's a long hard flight to the Bahamas each year but I'm
> leaving Mio today.

I'll spend the winter months in Eleuthera again and come back the first thing of May.

Fryer said the song has been played on a few radio stations, but the compact disc, which includes songs about other endangered animals, has sold sparingly. Still he occasionally plays it for his own children while they are in the car because it helps them understand what it takes to be a good steward of the environment.

A third song about the Kirtland's warbler has been performed by Darryl Saffer and Mindy Wilder on a CD called *Through Our Eyes*, released in 2000. A New Age instrumental piece produced as part of the Dan Gibson's Solitudes series combines the Kirtland's warbler song with soothing music. It's the kind of thing you might hear in a spa during a massage. All four pieces are available from iTunes and Amazon.com.

From orchestral music to pop tunes, birds have inspired hundreds of vocal songs and instrumentals. Some of them, such as Michael Jackson's version of "Rockin Robin" or "Blackbird" by the Beatles, have sold millions of copies. But like the Kirtland's warbler itself, it appears that Lonnquist's and Fryer's songs are likely to remain rarities.

PART THREE : *The Future*

THIRTEEN : At a Crossroads

Two million years.

According to geneticists, that's about how long the Kirtland's warbler has been occupying Earth as a distinct species.

Pause and consider for a moment the challenges the Kirtland's warbler has seen and overcome during that period: incredible variations in the North American climate, including four glacial periods that would have caused the warbler's current summer range to be under vast sheets of ice and its current winter range to be under water; mass extinctions, including those of the woolly mammoth, mastodon, giant sloth, saber-toothed cats, and giant beavers; volcanic eruptions and meteorite strikes, which caused sudden dramatic fluctuations in weather patterns; the rise and fall of sea levels, which allowed salt-water creatures to exist in the Great Lakes; and the arrival of Native Americans and eventually Europeans.

The Kirtland's warbler still exists as a species today because of human intervention, but the species itself deserves some credit for being one plucky bird.

Unfortunately, surviving multiple threats over the past two million years doesn't necessarily mean that the Kirtland's warbler's future is assured. Just as challenges evolved over that time and the warbler evolved to meet them, new challenges are ahead. Scientists warn that two insects that are not native to Michigan are expanding their ranges and are poised to do serious damage to the jack pine habitat. Other scientists warn that climate change in the coming years could put the warbler in jeopardy by changing its summer nesting habitat radically or raising sea levels, which could put much of its winter habitat under water. Certainly the most pressing issue for members of the recovery team is the day in the not too distant future when the Kirtland's warbler is removed from the Endangered Species List. If that happens and federal dollars for habitat support and cowbird trapping are removed, the warbler could go into yet another population tailspin.

What's a warbler to do?

From his office in Mio, Phil Huber of the Forest Service sees the warbler flourishing in the Huron National Forest and on nearby state land, but he's still worried. Even though the 2010 census found 1,773 singing males,[1] which is above the goal of 1,000 nesting pairs set in the 1974 recovery plan, Huber says the population is still small and therefore vulnerable. A crisis or a single event in the forest or on the wintering ground could change the warbler's fortunes in a heartbeat. Therefore, it's still necessary to be vigilant.

Huber sees two potential threats to the nesting grounds on the horizon: the sirex woodwasp from the east and mountain pine beetle from the west. An infestation of the wasp has the potential to damage the forest. An infestation of the beetle has the potential to wipe it out.

The sirex woodwasp is a native of Europe and Asia that came to North America in 2005 in shipping crates. From western New York state, it spread west into Pennsylvania and Ontario in 2006 and into Michigan in 2007. Before coming to North America, the wasp had already spread to Australia, New Zealand, and South America, where it has done major damage to pine plantations.

Unlike native North American wasps, which attack only dead or dying trees, the sirex woodwasp attacks living trees that are merely stressed or damaged. The female drills its ovipositor into the outer sapwood and then injects the tree with her eggs and a cocktail of a fungus and toxic mucus. The fungus and mucus act together to create a suitable environment for larval development inside the tree, but that mixture also eventually kills the tree. A single female can lay as many as 450 eggs.

Foresters appear to have two options for controlling this woodwasp. Because the insect prefers to attack weakened trees, foresters can protect healthy trees by removing less than vigorous trees before the insects become established in a plantation. Second, the Forest Service is experimenting with a biological control in the form of a nematode that parasitizes and eventually kills the wasp's larvae. The problem with the nematode is that it also is not native to North America and foresters are uncertain if its introduction will have an unintended impact.

A more significant threat to the jack pine forest is the mountain pine beetle, a native of western North America. These beetles killed millions of acres of pine trees in Colorado, Wyoming, Montana, British Columbia, and Alberta in an outbreak that started in 2007 and lasted through 2010. Foresters in Michigan fear that the insects will work their way east across the Canadian taiga to eventually enter and wipe out to the pine forests of the northern Great Lakes. Based on the damage done to millions of acres of western forests, the mountain pine beetle has the potential to do far more harm to the Kirtland's warbler's nesting grounds than the wasp.

The mountain pine beetle kills trees by boring through the bark into the tree's phloem layer to feed and lay eggs. Trees respond to beetle attacks by increasing their resin output to discourage or kill the beetles. Pine beetles, however, have developed a countermeasure to the tree's defense, carrying a fungus that blocks the tree's response. Shortly after the fungus enters, the tree starves to death because the phloem becomes too damaged to transport water and nutrients to the limbs. Previous outbreaks have often been mitigated or controlled by cold winters, which kill the beetles and limit the damage. Unfortunately, the 2007–10 outbreak coincided with a stretch of winters with above normal temperatures. Those warmer winters allowed larger numbers of the mountain pine beetle to not just survive the cold but attack trees at higher altitudes. Although no one is certain when or if the mountain pine beetle will arrive in Michigan, foresters are bracing for it.

And foresters might not be able to rely on cold winters to limit the impact of the beetle if the predictions about a coming change to the northern Michigan climate come true.

Because the Kirtland's warbler is so rare and has specific nesting demands, scientists worry about what will happen if the average temperature of its jack pine habitat increases by two degrees Celsius or if the climate grows drier, as some models predict. What will happen if the jack pine habitat across Wisconsin, Michigan, and Ontario dies out as a result of the increased heat and drought?

The first attempt to predict the future of the Kirtland's warbler came in a 1991 article published in the journal *Biological Conservation*.[2] That article used the Kirtland's warbler and its jack pine habitat as an example of an endangered species that was threatened by climate change and wondered if the jack pine habitat could be monitored as an indicator of climate change. If it were found that climate change was indeed having a rapid impact on the habitat, could management plans for endangered species change quickly enough to prevent extinction? Although no specific year was mentioned, Daniel Botkin, the article's primary author, wrote in a 2007 article in the *International Herald-Tribune* that his computer model predicted the Kirtland's warbler would be extinct by 2010.[3]

Botkin's article was not greeted warmly by many environmentalists, wildlife biologists, and members of the Kirtland's Warbler Recovery Team, who say it made bad assumptions about Kirtland's warbler's population dynamics and, more important, that it questioned why we should spend additional money on endangered species if they are going to die out anyway.

Botkin disagrees vehemently with those interpretations because he believes they are reading too much into the article.

Kimberly Hall, a climate change scientist with the Nature Conservancy's Michigan Field Office, also believes some people have attacked Botkin's article because they misinterpreted it. Hall believes the intent was to argue for a reconsideration of the way we spend money on endangered species and is a good starting point for examining climate change in the jack pine. Given that very few people are studying how climate change may impact endangered species, Hall wonders if we need to have a better understanding of what individual species are facing before we commit to spending more money on them or their habitats.

Hall cautions that it is impossible to make a blanket prediction about the jack pine growing in northern lower Michigan because there are so many microclimates in the Kirtland's warbler nesting habitat that it's possible that trees might die in one place but thrive only a short distance away. Nevertheless, the Kirtland's warbler occupies a habitat that is at the extreme southern end of the jack pine's range. Therefore, a warmer average temperature and drought could wipe out the jack pine in this portion of its range by killing the youngest trees before they are able to establish a root system deep enough to draw sufficient water to sustain them through drought and additional transpiration.

Stress from drought and additional transpiration would also likely have an impact on mature trees by stressing them, making them more susceptible to damage from native insects, such as the spruce budworm, and invasives, such as the mountain pine beetle and the woodwasp.

If the jack pine forest does start to die out at the southern end of its range, the Kirtland's warbler may be forced to shift its range farther north. Already a few Kirtland's warblers are nesting in Michigan's Upper Peninsula, and the Michigan DNR and the Forest Service are creating new areas of habitat in Baraga and Marquette counties. It's also possible that the Kirtland's warbler would shift even farther north, into Ontario, since there are areas with the right combination of young, patchy jack pine and sandy soil north and east of Lake Superior.

Ken Tuninga, a species at risk biologist with the Canadian Wildlife Service, says biologists now annually search for Kirtland's warblers in an area near Chapleau, Ontario, because that area is very similar to Kirtland's warbler habitat in Michigan. So far no Kirtland's warblers have been found there.

Although no significant changes have been recorded in the jack pine yet, a drier habitat could bring a positive trade-off: the jack pine would grow more slowly, and Kirtland's warblers could occupy nesting habitat for more years, lessening the need to create new habitat. It could also mean more fires and more Kirtland's warbler habitat created naturally.

Climate change could also alter the wintering ground in the Bahamas through increased drought, loss of habitat due to sea level rise, and more intense hurricanes. One climate model predicts an increase in the occurrence and severity of summer droughts, which means there would be less fruit and fewer arthropods for the warbler to consume.

Scientists also worry that climate change will bring about an increase in the frequency of the most powerful hurricanes—those that are considered to be category 4 or 5 on the Saffir-Simpson Scale. Joe Wunderle of the Bahamas research team says that a hurricane's high winds can not only strip fruit right off a plant but can also cause considerable plant mortality from salt spray and flooding caused by storm surges.

It takes a few years, but the plants and arthropods do return to a hurricane-damaged area, and wild sage, snowberry, and black torch—which provide fruit important to the Kirtland's warbler's diet—are among the first plants to grow. And, although it is possible that a powerful hurricane could kill some Kirtland's warblers, the winter population seems to be spread across many islands and a very wide area of the Bahamas and it's unlikely a powerful storm would hit all the birds in the same year.

As in Michigan, there also appears to be a trade-off: over the long term, stronger hurricanes could end up creating additional Kirtland's warbler habitat.

Temperature changes could also affect food availability not just on the wintering grounds but along the Kirtland's migratory path because models predict that temperature changes will not be uniform along the way. Some areas will be cooling, while others will be warming. That means that stopover areas in spring may have less food because of colder temperatures, while those same areas may have less food in the late summer because of drought.

The Kirtland's warbler is not alone in this boat. Terry Root, a biologist at Stanford University, predicts that one impact of the coming climate change will be that humans will be forced to decide which species will survive and which will go extinct. Root refers to this concept as "species triage," a reference to the process used by medical professionals to determine the priority of treatment based on the severity of a patient's condition, taking into account limited time and resources.

Given that it often takes thousands of years for species to adapt and the ongoing temperature increase is relatively sudden, many species will be unable to survive under new conditions. Root says that of the Earth's current two million or so known species, as many as four hundred thousand are expected to perish.

It may sound like species triage is a coldhearted approach, but Root says we are already doing something similar by deciding which species will be treated as endangered. In the future, government and non-profit environmental organizations will be forced to make more decisions, and with increasing frequency, about which species they will try to save and which ones they will let die out.

The Kirtland's warbler's chances for survival are increased because we already know so much about the species' habitat needs—much more than what we know about many other species, Root says. That knowledge is offset, however, by the warbler's habitat demands, of course, which makes it much harder to help the species.

Although the members of the Kirtland's Warbler Recovery Team don't live in a "what-if" world, they have begun to plan for a scenario that now appears likely: the day in the not too distant future when the Kirtland's warbler is no longer considered an endangered species.

Once a species is placed on the Endangered Species List, it is likely to dwell there for a very long time—perhaps forever. Of the 1,058 plants and animals on the list, only 47 have been removed. Some have come off because they went extinct, and others were removed because it was later discovered that their populations were healthier than originally thought. Nevertheless, only 20 species have been removed from the list because their population has sufficiently recovered, and not one is considered to be a conservation-reliant species.[4]

The Comprehensive Conservation Plan for the Kirtland's warbler, written in 1976 and updated in 1985, called for establishing a minimum population of a thousand pairs on the traditional breeding grounds. With the Kirtland's warbler's population now exceeding that objective and the conservation plan in need of updating, the U.S. Fish and Wildlife Service, U.S. Forest Service, and Michigan DNR are taking preliminary steps to take the Kirtland's warbler off the Endangered Species List.

Would that be the equivalent of throwing the Kirtland's warbler to the dogs? There is no provision in endangered species law that requires any kind of safety net or protections for a conservation-reliant species, and that means the state and federal dollars that fund the creation of new habitat and cowbird trapping could suddenly be cut off. If that were to happen, the Kirtland's warbler population could go into a downward spiral and end up back on the list.

In preparation for delisting, recovery team leader Carol Bocetti spent three years working behind the scenes to create an endowment or trust fund—a Kirtland's warbler safety net—that would ensure that there would always be money to fully support conservation efforts and protect the warbler in perpetuity. Such funds are common among wildlife conservation and hunting groups—Ducks Unlimited is a well-known example—but it is novel for an endangered species.

"These are conversations that we've never had before—no other [recovery] team has ever had before," Bocetti said.

Seed money and much of the planning for the trust fund are coming from the National Fish and Wildlife Foundation (NFWF), a nonprofit foundation created by Congress in 1984 that directs public conservation dollars to pressing environmental needs and matches these investments with private dollars.

The idea to create a trust fund for the Kirtland's warbler was introduced by Donn Waage, the director of the Central Partnership Office of the NFWF. Waage had been following the progress of the warbler and had been thinking about proposing an endowment fund for some time. He decided in 2008 that since the warbler was prospering it was time to start thinking ahead. He then approached the Kirtland's Warbler Recovery Team to assess its interest in a project.

Waage's interest in a Kirtland's warbler project came as a result of an internal reassessment of NFWF's efforts that concluded it was time to change its strategy. As a result of the reassessment, NFWF's leadership team concluded that even though the organization's accomplishments—helping to fund the recovery of the grizzly bear, whooping crane, and several species of fish and turtle—were impressive, it would be better if they were considered in a more holistic way. To be more effective, they concluded, the best way to spend their time, effort, and money would be to focus on habitats and species where their efforts could make a critical difference. The foundation has labeled these efforts "keystone initiatives."[5]

After NFWF designates a keystone initiative, it develops a business plan and lays out goals: what needs to be done; how it will be done; how much it will cost; and, perhaps most important, who will pay for it. Because NFWF relies on private money to match public money in all of its initiatives, the business plan helps potential corporate donors understand NFWF's conservation goals and the steps that will be taken to reach them. It has committed four hundred thousand dollars to the project and is seeking matching funds from private partners, says John Curry, assistant director of NFWF's regional Central Partnership Office in Fort Snelling, Minnesota. None of NFWF's money can be spent, however, if it is unable to find private dollars to match its contribution.

Curry says several steps will need to be taken before the species can be delisted, but the first step has already been accomplished. The Michigan DNR, the U.S. Forest Service, and the U.S. Fish and Wildlife Service have already signed a memorandum of understanding that defines each agency's role in future Kirtland's warbler conservation efforts. With that step accomplished, the three agencies have turned their attention toward creating a new and very specific conservation plan for the Kirtland's warbler. That plan will commit each to certain responsibilities based on the current knowledge of the species needs— such as maintaining a certain amount of acreage in nesting habitat. Concurrently, with the agencies negotiating that agreement, Curry is raising money and gathering names of potential leaders of a Kirtland's warbler "friends" group that would administer the trust fund and distribute money to pay for continuing habitat work and cowbird trapping. Although this group will ultimately decide its own role, Curry says he can see it taking over cowbird trapping and maybe even running the Kirtland's Warbler Festival or birding tours. To accomplish all of this, however, he estimates the group will need to build a twenty-million-dollar trust fund.

Of course, these developments are taking the recovery team into new territory, and now team members are talking as much about partnerships as they are about conservation. Bocetti, however, is ready for this next step.

"I think just from an environmental philosophy, this is a cool story," Bocetti said. "I don't think we're done telling it, either. I think we're going to lay some precedent down here in the next couple of years."

As positive as all these developments are, there is a bittersweet aspect to them, too, because when the warbler is taken off the Endangered Species List the recovery team's work will be considered complete and it will be disbanded. Without the recovery team, Bocetti will lose her connection to her friend in the forest. She is, however, okay with that.

"The goal of an endangered species biologist is to no longer be needed," she said. "That's what we live for."

Epilogue

Bill Irvine's first encounter with the Kirtland's warbler came when he was a senior at Michigan State University in 1951. He was not impressed.

Irvine was a forestry student on a field trip to the Higgins Lake area in northern Michigan when he was given a chance to tag along on the first Kirtland's warbler census. He had heard about the bird in class, and the census offered him not just a chance to see the bird but to learn more about the jack pine forest.

But on seeing his first Kirtland's warbler, Irvine paused and thought, "That's it?"

He may have been unmoved at the sight of his first Kirtland's warbler, but after he took a job with the U.S. Forest Service in the Huron National Forest in Mio in 1965, he had an epiphany.

"I spent as much time as I could wandering around the forests to familiarize myself. One day I ran into a man in a suit. He was an airport consultant from New York City who had been in Flint on business and had some extra time so he came up just to see the Kirtland's warbler," Irvine said. "He had heard one sing and was stalking the bird—moving in on it. Before too much longer we were joined by an elderly couple from British Columbia and another couple from New Jersey. That's when I realized that this little bird is an important part of the fabric of this forest."

So what is it about the Kirtland's warbler that attracts people?

Clearly there is no one answer to that question, but how you answer may just depend on who you are.

Members of the general public may indeed find the Kirtland's warbler to be charming and attractive, but mostly they come to see it because it's rare.

That's what lured Stan Brunton, a birder from Southampton in England, to northern Michigan. Brunton has traveled throughout the world to look at birds. Immediately after taking the Kirtland's warbler tour out of Grayling, Brunton will be off to Point Pelee National Park in Ontario to look for spring migrants, and from Pelee he plans to go to New York City to bird-watch in Central Park. Without the Kirtland's warbler, he says, there is no reason to visit northern Michigan.

Mike and Stephanie Garber came to the Kirtland's Warbler Wildlife Festival from their home in Nyack, New York, as part of a driving tour that combined birding, architecture, public gardens, and museums. Stephanie, an architect, wants to see the Kirtland's warbler because it will be an important addition to the list of birds she has seen, but she admits that she is drawn to the bird by its unusual nesting behavior. Mike, meanwhile, carries a Canon camera with a long lens off each shoulder. In his retirement years, Mike has remade himself from the administrator of a nonprofit corporation into a professional photographer. Some of his nature photos have been displayed in New York City galleries, and he wants to take a photo of the Kirtland's warbler suitable for framing.

Not long after walking down a desolate Ogemaw County road, a male Kirtland's warbler pops up and sits in the open on a jack pine branch only a few feet away. Mike snaps several photos, including one with the bird's head thrown back and mouth wide open in full song. It's a special moment, and the Garbers grin gleefully.

Rita Halbeisen, a biology teacher in Springfield, Massachusetts, has been drawn back to Michigan to participate in the annual census. She admits that she should be in the classroom this week, but she also says that this time in the field will make her a better teacher. Halbeisen grew up in Detroit with a love of birds and learned everything she could about the Kirtland's warbler as a child.

"I just know I was totally keen on the bird before I even saw it," she says.

As an ornithology student at the University of Michigan in the early 1980s, Halbeisen participated in the Forest Service's census as a seasonal worker. Now, as a teacher, she comes back every few years to participate in the census and reconnect with the Kirtland's warbler because "he's charming and energetic; he's just a wonderful little bird."

More than one thousand people, like the Garbers and Brunton, take the Kirtland's warbler tours every year because they have a great appreciation for birds and know that this one is different and special, says Phil Huber of the Forest Service.

"How many species of deer are there in Michigan? One. Bear? One. But there is a lot of variety to birds," Huber says. "That's what attracts people. And this one is particularly interesting because it is rare and it's attractive and it has a beautiful song. And there's something about traveling to a place to see something that occurs only one place in the world."

Indeed, if you want to see a Kirtland's warbler you still pretty much have to come to Michigan—good luck finding the forty or so birds in Wisconsin and the six or so in Ontario.

Ron Austing, a professional wildlife photographer from Dillsboro, Indiana, has taken wildlife photos all over the world and has had his work appear in books and national magazines. Although Austing is best known for photographing raptors, especially saw-whet owls, he admits that he is drawn to the Kirtland's warbler more than any other bird. At the age of eighty, Austing and his assistant, Bonnie Borisch, make the nine-hundred-mile round-trip drive to Michigan from his home in southern Indiana at least four times a year—twice for recovery team meetings, once for the Kirtland's Warbler Wildlife Festival, and once again later in the spring to take more photographs.

Austing took his first Kirtland's warbler photos in 1969, before the species was declared endangered and nesting areas closed off. After years of photographing birds from behind a blind, Austing came away amazed and fascinated at how tame the Kirtland's warblers were and how easily a human could walk right up to a nest.

Austing didn't get another opportunity to shoot more photos of Kirtland's warblers until the early 1990s, after he had retired from his job as a park ranger in southern Ohio. While driving home from Michigan's Upper Peninsula, Austing stopped at the U.S. Forest Service office in Mio to ask where he might be able to photograph Kirtland's warblers. Since all the nesting areas were closed, Austing was directed to a couple spots where males had territories that abutted a road. Austing says that while sitting on a roadside for hours waiting for a bird to come close enough to be photographed he realized why none of his better-known colleagues ever got good shots of Kirtland's warblers. Austing's patience and determination were eventually rewarded with amazing photographs.

In exchange for their assistance over the years, Austing has given many of his photographs to the U.S. Forest Service for use on their website and with educational materials for children.

"Even if I couldn't photograph anymore I would have to come up and spend time sitting and listening to its song," Austing says. "It becomes part of you. It's deeper than a simple click of a camera. I don't know how else to describe it. It's an emotional thing."

Perhaps those most deeply attached to the Kirtland's warbler, however, are the agency employees who have been tasked to save the bird. They have an unusually high sense of job satisfaction after watching the warbler respond to their efforts with growing numbers and expanded range.

In the early days of the DNR's efforts to create new habitat for the Kirtland's warbler, Jerry Weinrich helped to plant jack pine trees in the sandy soil of the barrens. A few years later he went back to those areas and found Kirtland's warblers singing in the trees. "When I look back on my career, that's one of the most satisfying things I can think of," he said.

Weinrich has an easygoing attitude, is quick to credit others, and doesn't put his emotions on display. But, said his friend and former coworker Ray Perez, when Weinrich talks about the bird, you can see the passion in his eyes.

"You have to have a drive and a burn," Perez said. "Jerry and I, we both had a burning passion. . . . It's a love affair with that bird and the habitat. If you love something bad enough, then you are going to work for it. It drove me and Jerry. It might have been something else. Who knows? It just so happened that this song, '*chur-chur-chur-chur-wee-wee*

. . .' If you don't hear it, you say, 'Damn, the forest is quiet. There's something missing.' The silence will hurt you."

On the other hand, Huber's attraction to the Kirtland's warbler is more spiritual than tangible.

"I think it's part of this wonderful creation that has been given to us," Huber said. "And it's worth preserving because of its mere beauty and because of the interaction between the animal and plants in the jack pine ecosystem."

In his time in Mio, he has listened to the stories of hundreds of people who have come from all over the world to see the Kirtland's warbler and concludes that many others are also attracted to it for spiritual reasons.

"People get a high off seeing such a wonder of creation," Huber said. "It's a work of art that can never be replaced if it ever disappears. And it's a fascinating machine. Could we invent something that weighs five ounces and flies back and forth to the Bahamas and sustains itself?"

Huber has worked closely with the Kirtland's warbler since his first day on the job as a biological technician fresh out of the University of Michigan in 1981. Since then he has seen both the low after the Mack Lake fire and the steady improvement of the Kirtland's warbler population during the 1990s and into the twenty-first century. And after thirty years with the Forest Service, he says that he continues to grow personally, learning more about the Kirtland's warbler every year.

For Carol Bocetti, her affection for the Kirtland's warbler comes from the two different roles she has played: as researcher, where she got to know the birds by their individual personalities; and as chair of the recovery team, where she is leading the effort to ensure the Kirtland's warbler is provided for well into the future.

Bocetti, Huber, Weinrich, Perez, and the many, many others who have had a hand in the conservation of the Kirtland's warbler have been through a lot over the years. They watched the Kirtland's warbler fall to the brink of extinction because of a lack of habitat and the impact of the brown-headed cowbird. They suffered through the pain of the Mack Lake fire and its aftermath. They made critical decisions based on guesswork and intuition—and to their relief discovered they were right more often than not. They have overcome challenges, fought through disappointments, and argued until they agreed.

The most obvious reward for their work will come in the future, when the Kirtland's warbler is taken off the Endangered Species List. Until then, their reward comes each May when they hear the song of the Kirtland's warbler fill the northern Michigan jack pine forest for another year. That's when they pause and smile and breathe a little sigh of relief knowing the Kirtland's warbler depended on them, and they did not let it down.

Then they go back to work.

Notes

INTRODUCTION

1. Spencer F. Baird, "Description of a New Species of Sylvicola," in *Annals of the Lyceum of Natural History of New York,* vol. 5 (New York: New York Academy of Sciences, 1852), 217.

2. *Auk* 3, no. 1 (1996): 144.

3. Frank Chapman, "Kirtland's Warbler (*Dendroica kirtlandi*)," *Auk* 15, no. 4 (1898): 288–93.

4. C. Hart Merriam, "Kirtland's Warbler from the Straits of Mackinac," *Auk* 2, no. 4 (1885): 376.

5. Francesca J. Cuthbert and E. A. Roche, "The Piping Plover in Michigan: A 100-Year Perspective," *Michigan Birds and Natural History* 15, no. 2 (2008): 29–38.

CHAPTER ONE

1. Blain's note appeared in the *Bulletin of the Michigan Ornithological Club* 4, no. 2 (1903): 63.

2. Frank M. Chapman, "Kirtland's Warbler (*Dendroica kirtlandi*)," *Auk* 15, no. 4 (1898): 288–93.

3. Ibid.

4. Norman A. Wood, "Discovery of the Breeding Area of Kirtland's Warbler," *Bulletin of the Michigan Ornithological Club* 5, no. 1 (1904): 3–13.

5. Ibid.

6. Ibid.

7. *Auk* 21, no. 4 (1904): 506–7.

8. Charles C. Adams, "The Migration Route of Kirtland's Warbler," *Bulletin of the Michigan Ornithological Club* 5, no. 1 (1904): 14–21.

9. Donald I. Dickmann and Larry A. Leefers, *The Forests of Michigan* (Ann Arbor: University of Michigan Press, 2003), 64.

10. Hal H. Harrison, *Wood Warblers' World* (New York: Simon and Schuster, 1984), 178.

11. Walter B. Barrows, "Editorial." *Bulletin of the Michigan Ornithological Club* 5, no. 3 (1904): 70–71.

12. Hal Higdon, *Leopold and Loeb: The Crime of the Century* (Urbana and Chicago: University of Illinois Press, 1999), 18.

13. James D. Watson, *Avoid Boring People and Other Lessons from a Life in Science* (New York: Knopf, 2007).

14. Nathan F. Leopold Jr., "Rare and Unusual Birds in the Chicago Area during the Spring of 1920," *Auk* 38, no. 3 (1920): 600–601.

15. Higdon, *Leopold and Loeb*, 6.

16. Nathan F. Leopold Jr., "The Kirtland's Warbler in Its Summer Home," *Auk* 41, no. 1 (1924): 44–58.

17. Ibid.

18. McGillivray would later go on to "real fame" as the composer of "The Home of the White-Tailed Deer, Michigan's Conservation Song."

19. Leopold, "The Kirtland's Warbler in Its Summer Home."

20. Leopold's comments on the Kirtland's warbler included observation of nest construction and location, nest cleanliness, and the way the bird hops while it is on the ground. He also made one keen observation into the warbler's habits that wildlife biologists and foresters would undervalue some fifty years later: "It appears that each male has a favorite perch, generally a dead branch of some description on a tree somewhat taller than the surrounding short jack-pine and to this he returns both before and after feeding, to sing." Who knew that a Kirtland's "favorite perch" would be so important? The Michigan Conservation Department clearly didn't when it began managing the forest for the Kirtland's warbler in 1958; favorable areas were cleared of all deciduous trees and jack pine trees were planted in thick monocultures. And then wildlife biologists wondered why the warblers didn't move in.

21. After Leopold's conviction, the state of Michigan banned the film on the grounds that it showed the face of a killer.

22. Nathan F. Leopold Jr., *Life Plus 99 Years* (Westport, CT: Greenwood Press, 1958), 171.

23. Nathan F. Leopold, *Checklist of Birds of Puerto Rico and the Virgin Islands* (University of Puerto Rico, Agricultural Experiment Station, 1963).

24. http://www.leopoldandloeb.com/letters.html, accessed October 16, 2008.

25. Ibid. Perhaps Leopold should have sent his display elsewhere. Repeated

attempts to visit it at Cranbrook have been met with silence by the museum's administration, leading the author to believe that Cranbrook no longer possesses it.

CHAPTER TWO

1. Harold Mayfield, "A Census of the Kirtland's Warbler," *Auk* 70, no. 1 (1953): 17–20.

2. Harold Mayfield, *The Kirtland's Warbler* (Bloomfield Hills, MI: Cranbrook Institute of Science, 1960), 129.

3. Harold Mayfield, Personal communication to Josselyn Van Tyne and Andrew Berger, June 25, 1956.

4. Leopold, "The Kirtland's Warbler in Its Summer Home."

5. Wood, "Discovery of the Breeding Area of Kirtland's Warbler."

6. Edward Arnold, "Another Nest of Kirtland's Warbler," *Auk* 21, no. 4 (1904): 487–88.

7. Leopold, "The Kirtland's Warbler in Its Summer Home."

8. Harold H. Axtell, "The Song of the Kirtland's Warbler," *Auk* 55, no. 3 (1937): 481–91.

9. Harold H. Axtell, "The Song of Kirtland's Warbler," *Auk* 55, no. 3 (1935): 481–91.

10. Mayfield, *The Kirtland's Warbler*, 125.

11. Lawrence H. Walkinshaw, *Nest Observations of the Kirtland's Warbler: A Half-Century Quest* (Ann Arbor: University Microfilms International, 1989), 71.

12. Leopold, "The Kirtland's Warbler in Its Summer Home," 56.

CHAPTER THREE

1. Harold F. Mayfield, "Brown-Headed Cowbird: Agent of Extermination?" *North American Birds* 31, no. 2 (1977): 107–13.

2. Janet Sullivan, "*Molothrus ater*," in *Fire Effects Information System*, U.S. Department of Agriculture, Forest Service, Rocky Mountain Research Station, Fire Sciences Laboratory [Producer] (1995), available at http://www.fs.fed.us/database/feis/, accessed December 3, 2010.

3. "Brown-Headed Cowbird, Life History, All about Birds—Cornell Lab of Ornithology," http://www.allaboutbirds.org/guide/Brown-headed_Cowbird/lifehistory, accessed December 3, 2010.

4. Harold F. Mayfield, "Vestiges of a Proprietary Interest in Nests by the Brown-Headed Cowbird Parasitizing the Kirtland's Warbler," *Auk* 78, no. 2 (1961): 162–66.

5. Walkinshaw, *Nest Observations of the Kirtland's Warbler,* 59.

6. "DNR—Kirtland's Warbler," http://www.michigan.gov/dnr/0,1607,7-153-10370_12145_12202-32591--,00.html#cowbirds, accessed December 3, 2010.

7. Lawrence H. Walkinshaw, *Kirtland's Warbler: The Natural History of An Endangered Species* (Bloomfield Hills, MI: Cranbrook Institute of Science, 1983), 151.

8. Walkinshaw, *Nest Observations of the Kirtland's Warbler,* 24–25.

9. Ibid., 34.

10. Andrew J. Berger and Bruce E. Radabaugh, "Returns of Kirtland's Warblers to the Breeding Grounds," *Bird-Banding* 39, no. 3 (1986): 161–86.

11. Walkinshaw, *Nest Observations of the Kirtland's Warbler,* 7.

12. "Yellow Warbler, Life History, All about Birds—Cornell Lab of Ornithology," http://www.birds.cornell.edu/AllAboutBirds/BirdGuide/Yellow_Warbler.html, retrieved September 11, 2008, accessed December 3, 2010.

13. Mayfield, "Brown-Headed Cowbird: Agent of Extermination?" 109.

14. Walkinshaw, *Nest Observations of the Kirtland's Warbler.*

15. Mayfield, "Vestiges of a Proprietary Interest in Nests by the Brown-Headed Cowbird Parasitizing the Kirtland's Warbler."

16. Mayfield, *The Kirtland's Warbler,* 28–29.

17. Recent advances in understanding the DNA of the Kirtland's warbler have rendered Sibley's conclusion outdated. Studies of Kirtland's warbler DNA show that it is among the oldest North American warbler species, perhaps two million years old or older, and it has no close relatives. Sibley asserted that the Kirtland's warbler's "present rarity" argues against its adaptability, but certainly the conditions on the North American continent have changed dramatically over the past two million years, and several species have developed or gone extinct during that period. In this respect, the Kirtland's warbler is not just a survivor but has thoroughly demonstrated its ability to adapt.

18. Harold Mayfield, "Where Were Kirtland's Warblers during the Last Ice Age?" *Wilson Bulletin* 100, no. 4 (1998): 659–60.

19. Elliot J. Tramer, "In Memoriam: Harold F. Mayfield, 1911–2007," *Auk* 124, no. 4 (2007): 1453–55.

20. Harold Mayfield, "A Census of the Kirtland's Warbler," *Auk* 70, no. 1 (1953): 17–20.

21. Richard O. Winters, "Cowbird Trapping and the Kirtland's Warbler," *Internet Center for Wildlife Damage Management, Bird Control Seminar* 6 (1973): 102–4.

22. Walkinshaw, *Kirtland's Warbler.*

23. Winters, "Cowbird Trapping and the Kirtland's Warbler," 103.

24. Chris Mensing, U.S. Fish and Wildlife Service, personal communication, 2008.

25. Walkinshaw, *Kirtland's Warbler,* 151, table 42.

CHAPTER FOUR

1. Jerome A. Jackson, "In Memoriam: Andrew J. Berger, 1915–1995," *Auk* 113, no. 3 (1996): 672–74.

2. Andrew J. Berger, "Experiences with Insectivorous Birds in Captivity," *Jack-Pine Warbler* 44, no. 2 (1966): 65–73.

3. Think that diet is odd? Berger wrote in one of his papers that he had had conversations with other people who raised captive birds, and they maintained that strained beef heart baby food was the "ideal meat food" for young birds. Andrew J. Berger, "Experiences With Insectivorous Birds in Captivity," *Jack-Pine Warbler* 44, no. 2 (1966): 65–73.

CHAPTER FIVE

1. W. Kim Heron and Bill Diem, "Forest Set Afire on a High Risk Day," *Detroit Free Press,* May 7, 1980.

2. Jack pine cones that have fallen to the ground have been known to open during extended periods of extreme summer heat. If the seeds germinate, however, they are unlikely to survive due to lack of rain and the competition from the well-established grasses, sedges, and other plants. "PLANTS Profile for *Pinus banksiana* (jack pine)/USDA Plants," http://plants.usda.gov/plantguide/doc/pg_piba2.doc, accessed December 3, 2010.

3. A. J. Simard, D. A. Haines, R. W. Blank, and J. S. Frost, "The Mack Lake Fire," U.S. Forest Service General Technical Report NC-83 (1983): 1.

4. "Huron-Manistee National Forest—Home/pages/Planning and Projects, U.S. Forest Service," http://www.fs.fed.us/r9/hmnf/pages/Planningand Projects/hfi/Fuels Specialist_Report_ 3_19_2003.doc, accessed December 2, 2010.

5. Simard et al., "The Mack Lake Fire," 2.

6. Dickmann and Leefers, *The Forests of Michigan*, 150.

7. Harold F. Mayfield, "Establishment of Preserves for the Kirtland's Warbler in the State and National Forests of Michigan," *Wilson Bulletin* 75, no. 2 (1963): 216–20.

8. Norman A. Wood, "In Search of New Colonies of Kirtland Warblers," *Wilson Bulletin.*

9. Les Line, "The Bird Worth a Forest Fire," *Audubon* 66, no. 6 (1964): 370–75.

10. Simard et al., "The Mack Lake Fire," 4.

11. Ibid., 13.

12. Ibid., 14.

13. Ibid.

14. H. Warren and P. Shellenbarger, "1,000 Flee Upstate Forest Fire; Blaze Kills 1 Man, Destroys 40 Homes," *Detroit News,* May 6, 1980.

15. Simard et al., "The Mack Lake Fire," 1.

CHAPTER SIX

1. Bruce Babbitt, "The Mio Model," *Defenders* 69, no. 3 (1994): 8, 36–37.

2. Barry D. Solomon, "Public Support for Endangered Species Recovery: An Exploratory Study of the Kirtland's Warbler," *Human Dimensions of Wildlife* 3, no. 3 (1998): 62–74.

3. Larry Leefers, "Economic Impact of Kirtland's Warbler Recovery Program," presentation to the Kirtland's Warbler Recovery Team winter meeting, March 10, 2010, Roscommon, Michigan.

CHAPTER NINE

The epigraph is from Harold Mayfield, "A Census of the Kirtland's Warbler," *Auk* 70, no. 1 (1953): 17–20.

1. Report from the Illinois Natural History Survey, published by the Prairie Research Institute at University of Illinois at Urbana-Champaign. http://www. inhs.illinois.edu/inhsreports/sep-oct97/migrants.html, accessed April 3, 2009.

2. http://www.nature.org/magazine/spring2006/features/art17202. html, retrieved August 25, 2008.

3. Bond was the inspiration for the name of Ian Fleming's suave spy, 007. Fleming was living in Jamaica while writing his first 007 novel, and he appropriated Bond's name because it was "brief, unromantic, Anglo-Saxon and yet very masculine." See "James Bond, Ornithologist, 89: Fleming Adopted Name for 007," *New York Times*, http://www.nytimes.com/1989/02/17/obituaries/james-bond-ornithologist-89-fleming-adopted-name-for-007.html?scp=1&sq=James%20Bond&st=cse, accessed May 20, 2009.

4. Bruce E. Radabaugh, "Kirtland's Warbler and Its Bahama Wintering Grounds," *Wilson Bulletin* 86, no. 4 (1974): 374–83.

5. Harold F. Mayfield, "Winter Habitat of Kirtland's Warbler," *Wilson Bulletin* 84, no. 3 (1972): 347–49.

6. J. Christopher Haney, David S. Lee, and Martha Walsh-McGehee, "A Quantative Analysis of Winter Distribution and Habitates of Kirtland's Warblers in the Bahamas," *Condor* 100, no. 2 (1998): 201–17.

CHAPTER ELEVEN

1. "What Is Safe Harbor? Conservation Incentives—Environmental Defense Fund," http://www.edf.org/article.cfm?ContentID=156, accessed December 6, 2010.

2. Paul Aird, "The Dispersal of the Kirtland's Warbler: Myths and Reality," in *At the Crossroads—Extinction or Survival: Proceedings of the Kirtland's Warbler Symposium, February 9–11, 1989, Lansing, Michigan* ([Washington, D.C.]: U.S. Dept. of Agriculture, Forest Service: [Cadillac, MI]: Huron-Manistee National Forests, [1989]).

3. Paul Harrington, "Kirtland's Warbler in Ontario," *Jack-Pine Warbler* 17, no. 4 (1939): 95–97.

4. Lawrence H. Walkinshaw, "Kirtland's Warbler or the Jack-Pine Bird," *Jack-Pine Warbler* 17, no. 4 (1939): 98.

5. Carol I. Bocetti, "Density, Demography, and Mating Success of Kirtland's Warblers in Managed and Natural Habitats," PhD diss., Ohio State University, 1994.

CHAPTER THIRTEEN

1. Michael E. Petrucha and Elaine Carlson, "The 2010 Kirtland's Warbler Census," *Michigan Birds and Natural History* 18, no. 1 (2011): 11–16.

2. D. B. Botkin, D. A. Woodby, and R. A. Nisbet, "Kirtland's Warbler Habitats: A Possible Early Indicator of Climate Warming," *Biological Conservation* 56, no. 1 (1991): 63–78.

3. "Science and Soothsaying/Daniel B. Botkin," http://www.danielbbotkin.com/2007/12/31/science-and-soothsaying/, accessed November 28, 2010.

4. "Delisting Report/Endangered Species Report; U.S. Fish and Wildlife Service," http://ecos.fws.gov/tess_public/DelistingReport.do, accessed December15, 2010.

5. Its use of *keystone* differs significantly from the way many biologists use the word. The foundation's use describes a critical species that will help scientists measure the quality of the habitat—a species that is a litmus test, if you will. If the Kirtland's warbler population suddenly drops, for example, NFWF and biologists will know that something is dramatically wrong in the habitat. Meanwhile, biologists already use the term *keystone species* to describe a certain species' disproportionate effect on its habitat. By its mere presence in this habitat, a keystone species helps to determine which other species will be present in the habitat. A Kirtland's warbler's presence in the northern Michigan jack pine forest has little or no impact on the presence of other species in the habitat.

Index

Page numbers in italic denote figures.